BREAKING FREE FOREVER:

Trails of a TRIUMPHANT *Woman*

CO-AUTHORED BY

TERRI ABBOTT

CHERELLE JEUDY

JOCELYNN MATTHEWS

RENARDA HARRIS

BRITTNEY KING

LATOYA JOHNSON

FOREWORD WRITTEN BY
DA'MALI GOINGS-RECTOR

Book proudly designed by RefinedConcepts.net

ISBN-13:978-1726133388
ISBN-10:1726133389

IN MEMORY OF
Jennifer Shenice Miller

A Precious Gift of Love from God!

And there I was standing still in the middle of this dental/medical lab trying to process why this woman kept saying and that's why we are destined to be friends for life. She doesn't even know me. She paid me no attention when I said I was good in the friend area. I was not trying to make friends. Already been hurt in that area. No Thanks!

Well who knew that was farthest from the truth. I was in need of a friend-better yet a sister in Christ. But I wasn't ready to let her know quite yet. It was something about her that made your frowns turn into smiles, your anger into laughter, your doubts into beliefs/because that just her. There was never ever a dull moment at work, not with Jennifer around. She wouldn't let it be that way.

I really enjoyed coming to work, things were turning around and promotions where present. The atmosphere was different and all of our colleagues were considered a "dream team" and Jennifer was effortlessly a huge part of the success.

I never had a sick day because she had remedies for everything. If you won't stop itching, have a migraine, mood was not good, had an upset stomach, blood pressure was high, no matter what it was Jennifer Shenice Miller had the solution.

Jennifer was a beautiful, loving, and kind person. She was also very protective of who she loved and would ensure that anyone coming up against that person would know not to mess with them. The person would have to approach you out of love or not at all. I was introduced to her family and they showed me so much love too.

For those that were special to her you would always hear her say "I love you to the moon and back".

Now I understand that Love is the key component that is what this world needs.

I decided to look up how far it was from the earth to the moon and Siri said it was 227579 miles one way. So I'm thankful to have been loved that much and Grateful to have received such a precious gift from God. Until we meet again!

Poem

My friend, No my sister!

My Friend, no my sister!
You always knew best;
especially when you were put to the test.

You are my angel, smart, funny and full of joy even when mad.
Jennifer, you were always a help in times Good or Bad.

You are the Sister I never had.

Our sisterhood shined through tests and trials.
We stood by each other and one of us smiled.

We wiped away tears and careful thought out plots,
which all seem so funny- Oh I miss you a lot.

And now that you are not in my presence I still count you sister and friend.

Thank you so much for the lessons I learned will last a lifetime.
And my love for my friend, no my sister will have no end!

- Sheena Moton

Jennifer,

As I gather myself to write these words I am torn between writing about how great of a mom, daughter, wife and friend that you were or write about how you are more than a conqueror through Christ with dealing with many health challenges and kept a smile on your face. I would have never imagined that I would need to write this about you because I never would have imagined you not being in my life.

You were the real MVP, Most Victorious Person, with how you dealt with life, health, and family. You were the epitome of greatness and knew how to smile through your pain. Your children and family adore you and whenever you were around the sun was always shining. You were a true light and likeness of the image of God. Nothing you went through stopped you for looking out for others. You were so selfless and the greatest aunt to my son. He adores you and always acknowledged you as "auntie". Now he has other aunts, but you were his favorite.

I am so grateful to have known you and experienced true love from your friendship and support with Julius. Only God knows why you decided not to tell your story, but I wish you would have. There are so many people who needs to understand life after 2 divorces, several brain surgeries, and challenges with her children. All I can say is remarkable, bold, courageous, fearless, and hopeful. I considered you an angel on earth, so when you made it to heaven I know that God was pleased with your life legacy. Thank you for loving me just the way I am, I really miss you so much but grateful for your time here.

Breaking Free Forever was your life. You broke free from the pain, hurt and fear of this life and entered eternity. God thank you for the life of my sister, she was a great example of if God is for us who can be against us. You showed your love through her life. Thank you so much.

Love,

Kimberly Gomillion

CONTENTS

FOREWORD

Dear Beloved,

Thank you for purchasing this book and investing in the lives of women all across the world including the co-authors who courageously shared their story through writing.

This book is about trials of a triumphant woman. A journey of women who have experienced illness, divorce, financial hardship, spiritual wilderness and much more but had the audacity to break free and change the trajectory of their lives. This book invites the reader to walk in familiar shoes but provides the strategies to overcome and live out greatness in the world.

The book is composed of writings from four women through the Breaking Free Forever IWrite2Heal program. These women have displayed great strength, integrity and character by coming together to share their life experiences with the goal of turning their pain into purposeful moments...sacrificing their time, finances and their hearts to dig deep and pull those painful moments from the root.

These women, Terri, Cherelle, Jocelynn, Renarda, Brittnety and LaToya have at least one thing in common; They have experienced life challenges and these challenges have held them hostage preventing them from living out their best lives at some point during their journey.

However, today they are living out their prefered futures now. They are not waiting for events and experiences to decide their fate but are deciding life on their own terms and declaring life to be fabulous and prosperously free.

No matter the style or technique of the writing of these women, each one of them has gone through a journey of discovery, acceptance and change and with any challenge in life, having the courage to acknowledge brokenness and the willingness to surrender themselves broken has been the most rewarding gift that any coach can experience and witness.

So, while reading their stories please take the journey too. Place yourself in their shoes and if their stories are familiar and you may have not reach a place where you are free from the things that have held you in bondage to your brokenness then use the tools and strategies to begin the healing process.

It is my prayer that as you walk through this emotional masterpiece, you walk through the peaks and valleys with the knowing that God's desire for our lives is to be healed, loved and reconciled unto Him.

These women can declare that they have "touched the hem of (our Savior's) his garments and now they have been made whole." (Matt. 9:21)

We encourage you beloved to get ready and touch the hem too! Healing is waiting for you and the world is waiting for you to break free forever!

In love,

Minister Da'Mali Goings Rector

Disclaimer

As a part of the program, each participant was required to submit a chapter in their own words. Each chapter you read will be the pure writings unedited version of their stories. Grammatical errors, spellings etc. is due to the authenticity of this publication. We celebrate each author for this major accomplishment.

New Millennial Christian Publishing

ACKNOWLEDGMENTS

"First, I give God the glory for everything! In my life, I have had many of situations that cause me to have a lot of sets backs. I was very disappointed with myself for a very long until I went to god surrendering and asking God for his forgiveness. After receiving God's love, I was able to accept the struggles, trauma and the pain of others after releasing it to God. Thanking a dear friend sister on trusting and believing in what God called her to do which was to help with the things I once struggle with. Sheena you change my life from pain to healing for eternal life. I thank you a million times, why because I trusted and believed in you. To all my children LeBria, Timothy, Nevillie, and Errol, mommy thank you so gracefully for putting up with the yelling and the fights, as I push myself through when I wasn't believing in my faith, Christopher, I just love given god all the glory for choosing me as your grandma, as you become a blessing to the family your love and presence speaks on a whole never level, so to say grandma loves her Motivation Grandson. To my sisters thank you for being there. Special S/O to the visionary Minister Da'Mali Rector for her spiritual eye of the Breaking Free Forever Healing to Writing Program. Da'Mali, becoming a part of the program it has taught me to break free from all trauma and I just want to say I thank you for my healing of being free forever! My mentor Kimberly Gomillion, you are what God calls Joy! I was a sign to you as my BFF mentor thank you for who you are and helping me in the process. To my #BFF Nation Co-Authors, Together We Stand We Made it!! To all family and friends thank you for your support!"

~Terri Abbott

✞✞

"First, I would like to thank my Lord and Savior Jesus Christ not only for this opportunity to share my story but for never leaving me or forsaking me. As I look back over my life, I know without a shadow of a doubt He was always there even when I felt alone, and I appreciate Him so much. Second, I would like to thank my husband, Emmanuel, and my boys for supporting me and encouraging me throughout the writing process and giving me the quiet and the space I needed to focus on this chapter. I love you all so much! Shout out to my sister, Brianna, and best friend extraordinaire, Camille, for helping me with editing. Thank you for understanding my vision and helping me articulate it clearly and authentically. Thank you to the visionary of this book, Da'Mali, for extending this opportunity to me. I pray you to continue to allow the Lord to use you to change the lives of many as you have changed mine. To my mentor, Keyonna, thank you so much for your valuable insight and for sharing those powerful videos. To my dear friend Sheena, I am extremely thankful for the words of life you generously share with me, you have gotten me through some really tough times just by a phone call. You are a gem. And finally, to my BFF sisters, my co-authors, Terri, Jocelynn, Brittney, Renarda, and LaToya, I love and cherish each one of you and I am so excited for each one of you. Be strong in the Lord, be fearless, and go change the world!!"

~Cherelle Jeudy

✞✞

"First and foremost, I have to give all honor, glory and praise to my personal Lord and Savior Jesus Christ, the author of my life. Honestly, I don't know what my life would be without him constantly breathing his breath into me. To my younger self, I remember you like it was yesterday. You did it baby girl! You pushed past the thoughts of yourself. Thank you for never giving up. You bring out the best in me. You are beautiful!

Amina McWhirter, mommy, thank you for creating a path for me to be a part of this book compilation. If it weren't for you knowing Ms. Da'Mali, I wouldn't have known about this opportunity. Thank you for pushing me to complete one of the many assignments of my purpose.

Dad, any man who can father me, is a very special man. Thank you for always reminding me that I can do anything I put my mind to and not to be worried about what others may think. Dad and Malissa, thank you for all the times you both let me talk your heads off throughout this entire process. Malissa, thanks for your continuous encouraging words.

My brother, Jr., you don't know how much I appreciate the encouragement of your words. You simply stated, "Jay, do your thing." I knew then that I made you proud.

Grandma Mary, tears start to flow when I think of you. I have no idea what life would be like without you in it. Your prayers, your scriptures, your love, and your talks pushed me to strive to do better. When I hear you constantly say, you are proud of me, I am reminded to keep fighting and defeating the enemy.

In memory of my grandfather, Robert L. Matthews. I never got the chance to even tell you about my book and becoming an author. But I pray I will continue your legacy and make you proud.

Mareva J., my best friend, I must say you showed so much patience throughout this entire process. Thanks for hearing my cries of frustrations and screams because I wanted to give up. You never ever let me quit! You kept reminding me that I could do this!!

BFF sisters, thank you for the sisterhood we have built. It was a process, but ladies we did it! I'm so proud of us all.

Ms. Da'Mali Rector, your spoken words continue to make a young adult like me listen to everything you say and everything you do. Your examples of passion and patience have impacted my life in a way that will last forever.

Sinetra Bowdry, thank you for professional edits and proofreading my chapter. Family and friends, thank you so much for all the support you have given. Always remember what I heard God say, "No one can you be YOU, but YOU. Have the FREEDOM to be YOU. I love you all!"

~Jocelynn Matthews

✞✞

"I thank you, God, first for giving the ability and wisdom to help me write this book. I appreciate my parents and grandparents for always supporting me in everything I do. I also like to thank my BFF Nation Ladies for supporting me also through this journey. I love everyone who's always been there with me and helping through the good, the bad, and the ugly. To God be the Glory!!"

~Renarda Harris

✞✞

"I would like to thank my heavenly father for never leaving my side as he continues to heal my heart. I have learned that we are not in control of our lives, but God has given us the power to respond to life challenges either destructively or with optimistic hope and blind faith!

I would like to dedicate my chapter to every women who may feel like giving up! Life can be a battle, but you must not fight the battle alone. Wear your armor of God daily in your life and put one foot in front of the other day after day. Eventually, you will be stepping in the right direction.

To my loving husband Girard King, I sincerely thank you for all your support during my writing journey. I thank my family for your unconditional love and your continued prayers. To the wonderful Life Coach, Da'Mali Rector. Thank you for your vision of a women's writing healing program as I have grown through this process. To my mentors and fellow Co-Authors, thank you for being patient with me as we are breaking free forever!"

~ Brittney King

✞✞

"First and foremost, I have to give God all the glory and praise for saving my life. I am nothing without you and I'm everything with you. Second, I have to thank and show my eternal grateful, love and respect to my A1 since day one, my mom Deborah Fair. I want to thank all the doctors, nurses and therapist who took care of me in P.G & Mt. Vernon Rehabilitation Hospital. Everyone who prayed over me and continue praying for me.

I also would like to thank my KIM Ministries family, Brain Injury Services(BIS) caseworker, staff and my fellow brain injury survivors, momma Candace and the Army of Angel's Auntie. The power of prayer is undoubtedly real and powerful.

I dedicate this chapter to everyone who supported me during this writing process, my BFF mentor and sister Sheena Moten. My fellow BFF author / my sister's, to my Total Life Changes family, Team Arise and Studio E-lan sister's. I have to thank my biggest fan Dewayne Ashby. I appreciate your love, support, encouragement and disappointments throughout this whole process. Also to the people who doubted me, who didn't believe in me, who hurt me and every tongue that rise up against me in judgement shall be condemned. Your hate is what fuel my fire.

Thank you Da'Mali for providing us with a larger platform to share our story. To my Godma Maurisette, I'm keeping my promise. Continue to rest in peace.

Thank you Coach Stormy Wellington, because of you, this chapter is possible. Thank you for reminding me, that these different events had to happen in my life. Thank you for teaching me the importance of speaking affirmations daily and always being inspiration. You are one of my sister's in my head.

Everyone who is in an abusive relationship, battling with depression or whatever issues you are facing. I pray that you found the courage you needed in this book and in prayer. To get escape and find peace. I'm praying for you, love you and God bless you all.

~LaToya Johnson

1

"SHE WHO STANDS ALONE!"
Terri Abbott

A woman with strength who believes in her power that helps her to overcome the negative trauma that kept her bondage.

Growing up in N.W., Washington, D.C. I was the first-born child to my parents, who was always amazing to me. Why? Because I was the only child at that time. Two years later, here comes a baby boy, my little brother, who I became the caretaker of. Next came my little sister, another child that I got to raise which made it so difficult for me because I was just a kid myself. Well, I had no choice because I was the oldest child and living in my parents' house it's their rules or no rules. However, I started to develop as a young woman at the age of nine, which made me grow up too fast. "Hmmm" I wasn't looking forward to what was about to happen to me "crying tears".

My life was changed once I became a victim of rape. "Fear, fear" I began to develop feelings leaving me scared to tell anybody because I didn't want them to say it was my fault. Yelling and crying with tears running down my face, I thought no one would believe me. Sad but true. I went home and told a family member about what just happened to me.

She looked at me screaming and yelling, "You got what you deserved."

"Why, because I'm the child with the attitude that Y'all call mean, grown and nasty? Who says that to a nine-year-old child? You are sick, and something is wrong with you."

She slaps my face, "Watch your mouth! I don't know who you think you talking to."

"Yeah okay," I said as I left to go to my mother's house. I never made it there because things weren't so great there either. I walked around trying to overcome the negative words that have already been said towards me. I felt like I just didn't want to live anymore. For days, I cried wanting to end my life. Thank God for my grandmothers who always prayed and had a heart for the Lord and would pray them demons off me. Having a little bit of support left me feeling guilty about being raped and left me asking why this had to happen to me. What did I do to deserve this?

Later, down the line, I was introduced to a 25-year-old man by my mother. Yes, my mother. You heard me correct. At that time, I was 13 years of age. I just came home from Children's Hospital Center after having surgery. I remember listening to my other family members yelling on the phone at my mother, saying that I was not going anywhere. Well, they didn't have custody over me. My mother had her rights in using her power to threaten me to leave. Leaving my grandmother's house and having to sleep with my mother's drug dealer was a lot. I remember crying telling my aunt, who knew him from her old high school. In addition to all of this, I just wanted to be a kid and go to school, but I felt like my life was robbed.

With me going through all of that, I was introduced to a Jamaican man who was standing outside on the pay phone talking to a woman asking my Elder did she need any help with her bags. My Elder responded, yes. He walked to the car while asking who the two young ladies were with her. Elder responded, "My daughter and granddaughter." So, he went on asking for our phone number and asked if he could take me out on a date at the age of fifteen years old. This man was older than my parents, which we later found out at his court date. "Wow" and surprising his age came out after he was in trouble with the law for drugs, and him needing someone to vouch and translate for him. So, guess what he used me because I was five months pregnant with his baby with no understanding why my life was set up this way. In 1994, I gave birth to my daughter at sixteen years old. "Now", I'm grown standing all alone after, my life was damaged. I was left to raise another baby on my own, but the only thing different is she mine and not my siblings. However, after dealing with all this trauma and negative impact I reached out to my grandmother who called me "Baby Girl". I would beam showing my pearly white teeth, loving when she calls me that. Hmmm, someone has a love for me. My grandmother always prayed and spoke life over me saying, "Baby you are God's chosen one and no matter what life brings, just remember God is in control." By receiving what my grandmother told me, I kept that close to my heart at the times I felt all alone in the dark when not many people were there. But, what amazes me is God never left my side not one inch and I am grateful to know that I have a relationship with God. Singing my favorite song that moves me every time, "What a friend we have in Jesus." "I am who God says I am!" A woman who believes in her spiritual powers that help her while she stands alone!

Becoming a young mother, I had to raise my daughter with this grown man that couldn't even give me a decent place to live, so I can raise her in a safe environment. However, I wasn't going to allow myself to continue to be brainwashed or traumatized mentally by my household. I would pack up and move from house to house, so my daughter wouldn't have to go through the same drama, trauma, and negative things I went through as a child. We went from house to house praying and asking God to watch over us while providing a safe, comfortable place for us to sleep, even when the family wasn't at their greatest in dealing with family issues especially when money is involved.

Experiencing the happy and ugly life, made me continue to be strong and believe that I can overcome the trauma. Telling myself to be happy and live, praising my good life in God's protection knowing that all things can be strengthened with my Lord and Savior. In addition to my only daughter, God blessed me with my oldest son. Now, I'm living on my own with two kids and working three jobs, doing hair to manage and pay my bills alone while taking care of my sick mother who was ill from HIV and coming to find out after 9/11 that I was eight weeks pregnant with my third child, who took me through some health scares while carrying him. Having to go through surgery all alone caused me to believe that it was just me and my kids. My mother was ill so there wasn't much she could have done, and my sister just wanted to finish school and enjoy her life as a young adult coming out of high school. Most importantly, my sister was able to go and live with my mother and brother after she graduated from high school and was willing to help care for her, which allowed me to focus on work and taking care of the needs of our mother. Next, my mother's sickness started to take a turn for the worse due to her body fighting for so long and waiting for some assistance, so she could get her medications that were required by the doctors. Now here I am sitting and watching her cry out in pain asking God to heal her or just take her away from it all. All kinds of thoughts were running through my head because of the amount of pain she was in. Crying in my room with the doors closed, I didn't know what else to do or how to help my mother. This made me want to end my life. At that moment I knew it was real because my family wasn't about sharing each other business most of the time. My mother didn't want her siblings to know because of the judgmental comments that have been said towards each other. This caused me to do everything on my own. Walking around carrying so much weight in my heart caused me to have depression, mood swings, anxiety, and anger. One day I found myself at my sister's house telling her that it was too much that I was dealing with and I was ready to end it all. I explained that it was so much going on, and I just felt trapped, and I was tired of living in darkness and wearing a mask like everything is okay. Calling the insurance number on the back of my card explaining to the operator what was going on she decided to schedule an emergency appointment, so I could speak to someone. Deep breath, I started calling on the name of Jesus. I then heard a whisper in my ear telling me that, "It's already done! Just trust and believe in His work." So, I did just what God said, I put my trust in Him.

Next, my mom called saying that she was ready to go home to be with her mother. Tears ran down my face and I heard myself screaming, "Why you are saying this?" She knew her reason because her sickness took a turn very fast. So, after her being in the hospital the doctors and nurses started to call saying that she is making great progress, and then later that night the nurse called and said she was not doing so well and things were not looking good. "What do you mean?" I asked. Receiving that call and being her oldest child, I knew that it would be hard for my siblings to deal with the loss of our mother. After my mother's death and being the oldest child, I had to be the one to care for my siblings up to their early adulthood life. Trying to get over the stress, I began to find myself partying in the clubs every day of the week, smoking weed harder than usual. At that point, it didn't feel like I had anything to live for even though I had my own kids. It just didn't feel right losing my mother.

After my mother died, there weren't many people I could trust to express my feelings. Dealing with older men for money was the thing for me and selling drugs was the way I survived at that time. I paid my way through the streets of D.C.

A lot of these men were very toxic when it came to relationships. I believed them when they claimed that they loved me, and they wanted the best for me after a great night of us having sex. Some of them thought they had my children mind caught up by thinking they cared about them because they were giving them things. Until one day God revealed something to me. While I was sleeping crazy, I jumped out my sleep looking for my kids. I would approach their rooms to check on them to see if everything was alright. I would praise God every time I found that they were sound asleep and safe. I began to walk through my house searching to see what the dream was showing me. I didn't find anything, but I received the message that God was showing me. It was not a godly thing to have these men around my kids that were not their father. Tears running down my face, I felt that it was his way of telling me to slow down because I didn't want that to happen to my children. The message was to stop exposing them to different men. However, my anger has changed towards a lot of things like me wishing that I was dead; believing the only one thing that I'm good for is trusting these men I'm sleeping with men that really didn't mean me any good. I decided to change my way of thinking that helped me to easily get over the thought that I had to use my body or to sell drugs to make it through life. I woke up one morning and began to pray to my Lord and Savior, believing and trusting that standing on the Most High's powerful Words is what protected me from the streets and not reliving the trauma and the abusive relationships that I once lived. Hearing from God nobody was going to trap my children in believing those lies, Terri didn't allow them to get comfortable with them. After, talking with God, the Holy Spirit started to speak and show me things how they cheated on me. Giving God all the glory for being with me every step of the way while I was out there trying to survive to take care of my family.

Being a single mother was not easy. It was hard for me because of the struggle of not having much support from either side of my family. Looking at my life one way, not finishing school and raising kids was stressing me out. Trying to come back around my family after the Leaders of the family passed away caused many arguments towards one another. Not really understanding why I noticed whenever I came around there was always a problem. In the process of leaving and creating space, I found out that they seem to have a problem with me all the time. So, I just keep my distance from everybody. After, seeing my Elder pass away, I began to really see how the family was towards each other. Asking God why he chose this family for me to be in where there is so much selfishness and hate in them. Finding my own love in the community, help me in ways to support my children when no one else did. So, I had to teach my daughter how to care for her brother's while I worked. Leaving them at times made me just want to quit everything that life had for me, because of the struggles of being a single mother. Going back and taking chances by selling drugs to keep food in the house and a roof over their heads left me feeling less than a mother. I cried lots of nights asking God to please come and help me change my life for my family. I don't want my children to be a part of the streets. God revealed to me that I had a talent for braiding hair, doing nails, etc.... (smiling). I didn't know that this was going to become my side hustle until people were really coming to get their hair and nails done. Now money was coming in and things started to look good for me to leave the streets for good now. I was able to provide for my household now. Then I became injured which left me not being able to braid hair anymore. I was devastated and spent months leaving all kinds of negative thoughts in my head. Stronger than I thought, I didn't turn back to the streets again. It was like playing a game on how much you going to make. Sitting on the side of my bed while on doctor leave, I made a promise to myself on finding a job looking for a better path to my future. After searching I found two jobs that called me in for interviews which change my life. One of the greatest moments ever. After receiving that call, I knew it was no turning back to the toxic lifestyle I was making for "Terri". God began to provide ways for me to have the income to pay my bills, food, utilities, and transportation to get to work daily. I eagerly accepted both jobs but felt like I was standing alone as I began to stress who could help watch my children while I worked both jobs. I called on relatives believing that they had my back while I worked. Crazy, that caused nothing but more problems than ever because of the hours I was scheduled to work. In addition to this, it was never understood if they were getting paid to keep them. I didn't understand why they complained. It was never a moment that I didn't pay or give someone something for the care of my children. It surprised me because I remembered their child care sitter was me. I missed out on my childhood enjoyment caring for them. Sad but true. So, I prayed and asked God to provide safety for my oldest child while she cared for her two brothers while I worked. After starting the job, guilt started to bother me. One night while driving home, I began to talk to God again about preparing me to have a conversation with my supervisor about the lack of childcare I was experiencing. After, speaking to her my children was able to come on certain days of the week. What's more than a blessing, I received that my kids would be in my care. I danced and praised God for his glory because my prayers were being answered, and I felt that my children and I were not alone anymore! Years, later things have started to come together my daughter was old enough to work a part-time job, which helped me out with small things in the house.

Watching my daughter grow up was scary for me because her father was not there to help most of the times when she needed him. Living the street life had become his home away from home causing him to lose out on raising his daughter. Many would say that he took good care of his daughter; "yes" he did when the mother had to pay up with sex behind closed doors. This left me feeling ashamed because the man that got me pregnant in the first place was charging me sex as a trade-off to take care of his own daughter.

I continued to "Stand Alone" after having my kids, and their fathers would leave me to raise them while going to dealing with the other women they were dealing with in the cut. Standing up to them, letting them know that these are their children and I am not playing the sleeping around game with the men that help make them. Never again.

Years later my two oldest made me the proudest mother ever, watching my only daughter grow into a young woman chasing her dreams and raising her son always put a smile on my face! Seeing them both graduate from high school, going to college, and watching how my son put in work playing football (which he was honored by receiving a full scholarship) made me very proud of myself. God provided for me to take care of them. Looking at my life one way and seeing how the struggle was I couldn't get to finish school due to the overload of stress that going on. I was hanging out with friends who claimed they were my true friend until things had gotten harder for me. Now it's no more so-called friends.

Lost woman crying out for her father after the loss of her mother. Crying every night asking God to please mend my relationship with my father. After many tries of reaching out to him, he continued to reject his grandchildren, other kids, and me (his oldest).

However, after not having the support as a little girl or a young woman, I still managed to love my family from afar. I went back to school and graduated from Roosevelt Stay with my high school diploma and then taking it to the next level by attending the University of The District of Columbia for my degrees. Proud of myself after all negative things I went through. I still had Christ to guide me to keep pressing my way. By going back to school, I was able to secure a better future for my family. I am proud that I was able to graduate in the year of 2016 with two of my children also graduating.

Later, I was told by the doctor that, I was borderline for diabetes nothing but grace and favor from God because he helped me to come down from 220 pounds. By changing my eating habits, it helped me stay on track with exercise regularly during the week. Seeing how fast the weight was coming off I noticed the shedding of the weight was down to 178 pounds and my goal was to reach my body mask weight which is 145 lbs. Losing this weight has really boosted my self -esteem towards so many things that I never thought I am serving wherever there's a need for God's work. Every night, I prayed asking God to give my father and I the relationship he desires us to have with one other. After the struggle of being a single mother trying to face the reality of not having anybody there, I just did what I enjoyed doing, which was singing and dancing. This would make me feel so good about myself causing the pain to be numb for a while.

Leaving me to bury my mother was the hardest thing a child could do. Having to deal with all this amount of caring for others help me recognize my passion for people. This is what makes me very proud of myself by having a gift to care for others. Glad to say that everything I went through helped me become the woman I am today!

Devotion

"Honor your father and mother so, you would have a long life on earth."(Ephesians 6:2) God's word speaks! Your parents may not be perfect in your eyes, but as a child of the Lord we must live in obedience of our parents because they are lord. As, we stand in the midst of our struggles, God speaks!

A final word, "Be strong in Lord and in his mighty power. Put on all "God Armor" so, that you be able to stand firm against all strategies of the devil." (Ephesians 6:10)

God did not put us on this earth to fight against our flesh and blood, but to stand firm against the evilness of the authorities of this dark evil spirits in your heavily places, homes, jobs, schools etc.

Just put one very piece of God's Armor on so that you will able to resist the enemy in the time of evil. Then after the battle you will still be standing still. (Ephesians 6:11)

Prayer

To God be the Glory! Thank you, for the bad, good and the ugly, that went on in our lives. Lord you said that you will never leave us nor forsake us and Father, your words are true that you'd never turn your back or change your mind. Father, thank you for the fruit of the children you blessed us to include our grandchildren. Thank you father for answering all of our prayers and what's more to come. Thank you for being connected to a circle of likeminded Christian women. Thank you father for giving us just one more chance to get it right, Father glory to your name for accepting us for who we are, and for allowing us to live again and again in your Loving Holy name Jesus.

BIO

Terri Abbott, a native Washingtonian of 41 years, is a mother of 4 and daunting grandmother. Terri is a small business owner of a brick and mortar t-shirt company and a rising professional speaker. She has built a social media platform (Facebook @Shay Shay Barracks, and Instagram @emarldbull) that allows her to inspire and encourage other women to be the best version of themselves. God-fearing, lovable superwoman, Terri enjoys spending time with her children and is very passionate about speaking/mentoring to the youth.

2

"JUST NARDIE"

Renarda Harris

You don't know my story, but everybody thinks that they do. You don't know what I've been through. Emotionally, Physically, Verbally and Mentally my mind is messed up. I grew up sheltered from everything even though I lived in different hoods I never experienced them. My mother always wanted me to have a good life. But what is the good life? I noticed something was mentally wrong with me in high school, but it wasn't because of grades or the type of school I went to. It's because I went from boy to boy, I don't know if it was daddy issues or not, but I do know one thing is true is that I didn't feel anything for them but except maybe for two of them.

I've been in love at least twice in my life, but my first love was what I thought was my everything. He was always a know it all. We were together for six years, but off and on. We used to argue like rapid. He used to call me names such as sluts or even hoes sometimes. After a while, I started thinking maybe just maybe I was after he kept saying it to me. But, me being young and dumb I took the verbal abuse and kept going back to him. HA! Wasn't I dumb for that? But, I believe it still didn't teach me anything. The summer of 2015 I went to go visit him and thinking everything would be good just how it uses to be. Well, we had talked and chilled and did other things for the first time. It was nice and passionate but then we started arguing when I told him I love him but can't be with right now. It was like a light that went off in his head and he pushed me against the wall while my dumbass was still begging for him. Then, he slammed me harder and harder, while I was crying. He threw me out of his house and called me a whore.

But, that was just some of the problems I had dealt with. I used to let guys use me in high school because I didn't know I was worthy of being with a real man. When I graduated I was so glad to be done with high school finally in 2013. I thought I was ready for the real world, but I was wrong. When I became 18 like, I just let loose because for my senior year I was in a shelter. I met a lot of memorable people there and I also met some that were there that had no self-worth. Anyway you can say that's why I was so ready to be out of there. I was happy when we moved.

One day, I went to the DMV to get a background check when I met this guy and he was so fine I was thinking in my head that, "I wanted him." We started dating in October of 2013 and I thought it was going to be something special. Well, my parents were not home, and we were alone together. What was so different about this day than the other days? It wasn't just how he looked at me. I was trying to chill and that's it, but you can tell he had other ideas. He used the famous line, "let me just put the tip in" but, at this time I didn't know what was going on. Yea, I know I was 18 but I still never had sex with a man until this point. My mother came in after he left, and she said, "it smells like sex." I said, "I don't know what you're talking about." Being with him made me sneak around and forget everything. I was 18, but my mother didn't treat me like I was at the time. This was the point in my mother and I relationship, which everything had changed. We fought and argued all the time after this point she couldn't see my views and I guess I couldn't see hers, but I just wanted her to treat me like I was an adult and she couldn't, which frustrated me to my core like I wasn't old enough to make my own decisions and mistakes. While we stopped dating because he didn't want more, and I was going to college in the spring of 2014.

This is when my life changed completely. I went to college for the first time as anyone would but for someone like me I do anything, and I did anything because I was so sheltered, so I lived when I got college. I did my school work obviously, but I also had fun and I mean so much fun. I started drinking excessively and partying when I first or to college. I met this guy who helped me to class one day because we had the same class, but little did I know what I was getting myself into. When the next semester came, I had my own room, and everyone told me own room, and everyone told me that he was bad news. My problem is that I never listen to anyone. Well, we were hanging out with each other on the daily basis for like three or four weeks. One thing that I learned is that college moves fast. I started to show interest in someone else and we started hanging out with more. One day, he came into my room and saw a hickey on my neck from the other guy. He got so mad that he started to turn purple. He pushed me on the bed. I told him to move away from me and get off of me, but I guess because I didn't scream it wasn't enough. He forced himself on me while tears fell from my eyes. He pushed and pushed as hard as he could first vaginal then anal. I wasn't on my cycle but all I felt was blood rushing down from my body. I laid there just crying after he left but before he left he says to me, "This is something you'll never forget." He was right! I went straight to the shower to clean up myself up while everyone thought I just got fucked and I let everyone believe it because I was scared to tell my truth. You think to yourself, who would listen to you? Or no one would believe you. Well, If I know what I knew then I would've told somebody. I was in so much pain then and not to say that I'm not still in pain because I think about that every day of life. He wanted me to remember it and I have because it's hard to forget about it. I wake up in tears, shaking sometimes because of what happened. I had to take counseling for months and still taking it. It has made me ruin relationships because I never thought I wasn't worthy enough for them or deserved to be happy because that happened to me. But, another reason why it hurts so bad is that I was pregnant after he put his hands on me. You may wonder what happened to the baby, or did I kill it? No, none of the above because I was going to keep the child but one morning I woke up, it was blood everywhere and I didn't know what to do. Whether to cry or just feel relieved? No one ever knew but my doctor of course and I never wanted anyone to know either.

It deterred me from being in a real relationship, but I waited a whole year and so before I got into a real steady relationship. He loved me and treated me right. I didn't know what it was like having a someone to be my friend and my supporter when I needed it the most. I didn't how to be a faithful girlfriend at times because I was still dealing with the pain of my rape and didn't know how to get attached. He showed me a different type of guy and he saw me when no one else could see who I was. I didn't care what people thought of us being together even though everyone had their opinions. For instance, my mother didn't approve of my relationship because he didn't have enough money for me in her eyes but it wasn't about the money for me, I've always been independent. It grew us apart even further but I know she's my mother and just wanted the best for me. My father didn't approve of our relationship either though he never met him, he only saw what he thought he knew. My father has always been protective of me but I didn't grow up with my father as much as I wish did and I was always jealous of my sister and brother because they lived with him and got to spend more time with me. My father and I connected more when I got in middle school and I know he wanted to do more because my father never thought that money was enough for me. My parents are both crazy individuals but there my family and would do anything for me if I need them. I know that they only wanted to just see me happy and I understood that but in my mind, I was happy to have this good man in eyes, yes we had issues but what relationship doesn't have issues. He prayed for me and before him, I never had that. I loved him but couldn't show it because of my own past and I was scared to open my heart all the way. He taught me what it truly means to love someone or to be loved. I trusted him, and he had trusted me, but life happens and gets in the way of relationships. We were connected and as one person sometimes. When we broke up it took everything from me and I broke down and lost myself during the breakup. I lost myself, but I gained the respect of the new Renarda and it made me stronger to get through it. During the breakup, I went through so much and it was one of the worst times of my life. I was so stressed out that I didn't know that I was pregnant and lost it. As tears fell down my eyes, I wanted to die. I took fifteen different pills; one pill at a time and slowly as my eyes were drying up and even my hand was shaking because after that I felt like I lost everything when it happened. I went to the hospital and they took care of me. Since we broke up my ex-boyfriend and I became friends so that we can get past everything in a productive way and he was there for when I was going my suicide attempt. Love conquers all sometimes and being friends with someone is sometimes better than blocking a person out of your life who I was connected with by something powerful, such as what we went through.

Well, at least I thought that my life was over even though my life was just beginning. I prayed every day and night. I went to church more after those hard times. This situation made me want to be a better person and turn my focus to God. I got saved because I wanted to find myself again and do more. I read the bible every day and took notes on the words that I read. I used to think that I wasn't strong enough to handle these things, but I learned that you can come back from the worst situations and get stronger from them. I asked God to forgive me for all my sins every day and that's all I can do. I went through heart attack last semester, but I got that energy and put all the energy into my studies. All the anger I had I put it into my work because with everything else going on I wanted to make sure that my grades were good. I focused on my education and working at the school to help me center myself because I'm the first to graduate from my imitated family. I'm proud of my accomplishments and I've been working hard to focus on myself because being the best Nardie is all that matters and all that I can be. But, let me tell you the devil tried to come into my life and ruin it at times but I'm not letting him get into my life. So, "Bye Devil and Get the Heck Out of My Life." My life is all about positivity and no negativity no more because life is too short to worry about the petty things in life. These experiences taught how to love again and that one day I can find the husband of my dreams but that I don't need a man to always be there for me. I've always been independent that's will always continue with or without a man by my side but God is all I need to get through any obstacles that come into my life. No more looking behind me just forward and ahead of me. I'm not letting any more barriers get in the way of my success.

Devotion

Prayer

I pray that this book helps to open doors for me and helps young women everywhere. I pray that this will be a great school year and I will pass all of my classes and focus. I hope everyone safe and protected and has lived their best life.

BIO

Renarda is an aspiring Social Worker and model, who desires to assist other young women to be comfortable in their skin no matter what anyone says and as a motivational speaker for the youth she will impact their lives with sharing her testimony. She is a graduate of West Virginia State University and is currently pursuing another degree at the University of the District of Columbia. After graduation, she desires to implement plans for her non-profit organization to help people around the world who are dealing with domestic violence.

3

"FACE THE MIRROR"

Jocelynn Matthews

Have you ever been afraid to look in the mirror? When you look in the mirror, what do you see? Well, over the years, when I looked in the mirror I saw myself as a dark skin, thick, nappy hair, fat stomach, no butt, big boobs, chinky eyes, four-eyes, and small ears girl. I never liked looking in the mirror. I thought I was the ugliest thing on earth.

As you read this chapter, remember to ask yourself the same two questions I asked myself. Have you ever been afraid to look in the mirror? What do you see when you look in the mirror? I want to take you on a journey. First, let me warn you. You are getting ready for a roller coaster ride of my emotions as I candidly display to you my mind's eye of why my self-esteem was low at such a young age. You may feel a little uncomfortable for the next hour or however long it takes to read this chapter, but, at the end, I pray that you will be encouraged, enlightened, and inspired. Therefore, I ask you again. What do you see when you look in the mirror? Perhaps, you cannot think anything at all. On the other hand, you may have good thoughts.

Reflection Question: Take some time to write your emotions down in the space provided below.

____
____
____
____
____
____
____
____
____

Webster defines mirror as something that gives a true representation. Definition number two uses the word, self-esteem. Definition number three uses the word, self-worth. Dictionary.com defines self-worth as the sense of one's own value or worth as a person. At an early age, when I looked in the mirror, I had identity issues triggered by life encounters, which led to my poor self-worth and poor self-esteem. This entire chapter is about my personal journey of what I saw in the mirror. The image I saw stemmed from my life encounters as a little girl in elementary school until today as young Christian woman. The purpose of this chapter is simple- face the mirror. As you read, I want you to feel my emotions as a young girl whose mind was tormented by the enemy's attempt to destroy my self- worth.

Self-worth and identity issues clearly have been barriers in my bloodline. Literally, when I told my mom what I was writing about in this chapter, she began to share with me she and my grandmother's past. My grandmother moved from South Carolina to Washington, DC in the first grade at six years old. She suffered with identity and self-worth issues. Additionally, I knew that my mom dealt with low self-esteem issues, but I didn't realize the intensity of her issues until I started writing this chapter. Her earlier school years were heartbreaking. At the age of six, she was discriminated against because of the color of her skin. Also, a family friend molested her. These traumatic experiences had an image impact on my mom. Clearly, image issues for the women in my family started early. Some would say it's a generational curse. One curse that I, Jocelynn, am determined to break.

Reflection Question: Are there generational curses in your bloodline that you desire to break? Identify them. Write it now.

____

____

____

____

____

____

____

____

____

My Early Years - The Weight Gain

As a little girl, I never talked to people. I wasn't friendly. I was really quiet. I still don't believe I acted in this manner, because, I am the complete opposite today. Hey, that's what I was told, so, that's what we are going to go with. At the age of three, I started dancing at a professional dance company in Maryland. At the age of six, I started taking prednisone (steroids) for asthma, which caused me to gain weight. Automatically, I felt ugly. I had to stop dancing due to the amount of weight I gained and my lungs just kept collapsing onstage and off. Emotionally, I began to hurt. I really wanted to dance. Yet, at such an early age, I faced weight issues because I needed to take medicine that inhibited my ability to dance. Dance was the only thing that made me feel remotely happy and that had been taken away from me.

My Elementary School Years - The Bullying

I went to two different elementary schools. I was bullied. Those years were my early memories of trauma in school. One day, I was out on the playground. A group of girls didn't like me. I remembered four girls jumping me. I lay there as one girl kicked me. The other screamed, "Nappy hair, nappy hair!" Thank the Lord a teacher was nearby and things didn't get too bad, but being bullied was not fun. As expected, the girls were expelled, but I will never forget that day. This incident was another blow to my confidence and self-esteem. I felt even worse than what I felt before.

People will hate you, rate you, shake you, and break you, but how strong you stand is what makes you. ~ Dana Chanel

My Middle School Years - The Insecurities

My parents enrolled me in a private school. I had to become familiar with a new atmosphere. Things in private schools were completely different from public schools. Uniforms, all black shoes, skirt that goes past your knee-middle finger length, and no big jewelry were a part of my daily attire. The school was smaller. The class periods were longer. You talked about the Lord. There were group lunches. There was no cafeteria, and certainly, no cafeteria food. You had to bring your own lunch. You attended chapel- so on and so on. Just when I was getting adjusted to private schools, my parents decided to get a house built. My dad was ready for us to move out of the neighborhood. Someone was murdered right underneath our house. We saw the dead bodies. Needless to say, I changed schools again. Back to public schools I go.

I digress. Remember earlier, I talked about reading the roller coaster emotions of my feelings? Well, here goes. By this time, I started my womanhood, meaning I started bleeding out my vagina. Yeah. I know-TMI. You'll be okay. Just keep reading. Oh, wait! Let me tell you the details. My grandparents, brother, cousin, and I were on vacation in Florida. I had on a pink and orange one-piece swimsuit. We were in the pool. Out of nowhere, I had a brown spot on my swimsuit in the area of my private part. My little brother, who is two years younger says, "You look like you boo-boo on yourself." I went to my grandma (miss her-R.I.P.) on the edge of the pool. She said, "Come on Jocelynn, let's get out the pool, sweetie. You started your cycle today." I said, "What's that?" No one ever talked to me about this or if they did, I don't remember. I didn't even know what to do or not to do about sex. It wasn't really talked about in my house. If it had been talked about, again, I don't remember. I'm a pk (preacher's kid). So, a lot of worldly stuff wasn't discussed, watched or listened to, but that's another book. WAIT!!! Why did I just tell y'all all that? Oh, right! I'm sharing about my pre-teen and middle school challenges. Also, I'm just trying to paint a vivid picture. If you ever meet me, you will understand these digressions (sudden changes in subjects).

Let's get back to the topic. I'm back to my middle school years where I'm back in public schools. In 2003, my life was moving upward! I got my first boyfriend, GG (not his real initials)! I was so excited! Someone finally liked ugly duckling me. I started growing boobs (SMH). I didn't have to wear uniforms. I had a boyfriend. I had friends. I was winning. I was enjoying middle school.

As for having a boyfriend in my little kid relationship, it wasn't that much we could have done. We didn't have cell phones. We didn't have cars. We lived in two different homes. We weren't hanging with each other. My parents were not happy about me going over to other houses or hanging out with boys. We had a school relationship. In your mind, I'm sure you are thinking. Why were you so pressed about this boyfriend? Why are you still dwelling on this story? My response is, "Boo, I'm setting the scene for you and making sure you realize that I was infatuated by this little boy." Still, I went home believing I was ugly.

My perception was off. I was tormented daily. I couldn't bear how God created me. As a dark skin girl, I felt bad. This feeling interfered with my relationships with friends. For example, I always had friends that were light skin with long hair. I, desperately, wanted to look like them. It seemed like the light skin girls always had boyfriends. I was always told they were pretty and beautiful. The whole time my little chocolate tail was feeling like the ugly black duck that couldn't quack. Simply put, I hated the way I was created! Why, Jocelynn? I'm sure that's what you are thinking. Right? The answer was pretty simple in my mind. Actually, the truth was that I had issues with my self-worth, which was defined by the image I saw in the mirror. This mindset left me constantly questioning. Why did God create me to be ugly? What's my purpose? Why was I even born?

Reflection Question: When others are around, have you ever felt that you are good enough, you are liked, or you are this cool person? Then, when you get alone, you feel like crap? It's kind of like wearing a mask or painting this picture that's not true. Seemingly, you are one person in public, but a completely different person at home? Write it down.

____

____

____

____

____

____

____

Because of my own low self-esteem, I needed validation from people who did not have the wherewithal to handle my needs. My boyfriend wasn't telling me I was cute. I grappled with the feeling that he agreed to be my boyfriend just to be nice not because he really liked me. Our kiddie relationship was what you would expect in middle school. He walked me to my classes. We hugged after school. He walked me to the bus and even gave me kisses on the cheek. Still, a void was there, because, I didn't love myself. I didn't know me. I just knew I was looking for validation from someone for some reason.

Reflection Question: Do you crave attention? Do you act out to be accepted? If you answered yes, write down what you have done in your life to crave attention.

____

____

____

____

____

____

____

____

____

I digress. It's crazy because my parents probably going to read this chapter. I'm sure they will say, "Our little girl was a mess. She thinks we don't even know."

Let's get back on topic. I found out that GG was in a relationship with my neighbor, Mona (not her real name). We lived in the same neighborhood and attended the same school. We favored. We both wore glasses and our skin was dark. Apparently, GG was looking to break up. Eventually, we did. My little heart was broken. Later, Mona went around saying I wanted to be her. That's why she was dating GG. Of course, with my struggles of self-love, this break-up had me thinking badly of myself. As a result, we had a fight. That night, I cried like a baby. I cried for multiple reasons. I got in trouble for fighting. I embarrassed my parents. Most importantly, I cried because this was my first heartbreak. In the end, I pulled myself together. I joined the step team and increased my grade to a 3.0 that school year. That was the end of public schools.

Reflection Thought: How many days or years have you cried yourself to sleep over something or someone? Maybe you had a thought that nothing would go right for you after those tears had fallen? YET, you are still here. Right? You are living your life to the fullest! Yes, there is purpose on the inside of you. My pastor always says, "What you go through has nothing to do with you. It's for someone else." So our sleepless and crying nights are for a reason- to help someone else. Don't give up. Keep living!

Keep away from people who try to belittle your ambitions. Small people always do that, but the really great people make you feel that you, too, can become great. ~Mark Twain

Reflection Question: Write what you feel like you faced that will eventually impact someone else. This is kind of like a reminder of what God did for you.

____

____

____

____

____

____

____

____

____

The High School Years - Strange Mentoring

I attended three different high schools - two private and a year of homeschool. Turning sixteen felt like a teenager's dream. Well, mine started off amazing. I had a sweet sixteen party gifted to me by my parents. I had my hair and nails done, but I hated my outfit. It was a glitter half sweater with a black shirt and blue light jeans with black glitter. My house was decorated nicely as a courtesy of my Aunt Felicia. She set it up so fly. I had a red carpet, paparazzi, cardboard celebrities, a DJ, and a lot of people. I felt like a Princess. Princess Jocelynn was partying like it's 1999. You couldn't tell me I wasn't cute that day. All eyes were on me. I sweated my Mohawk out and make up off. A week later, my party pictures come back. I looked at everyone in the pictures and gave them all compliments. In my mind, I was the ugly one in the picture. Instantly, I spiraled back into self-hate. I cut up the pictures. I talked negatively about myself. I called myself fat. Everyone else's outfit was cuter than mine. Then, I started to be envious of my friends. I hung around one girl more than others only to study her. I wanted to be like her. Oddly enough, I hated her because I wanted her life. Eventually, we became friends. That's when I realized her life wasn't that wonderful.

Reflection Question: Have you ever wanted someone else's life to be your own? Write down what was so amazing about their life.

____
____
____
____
____
____
____
____
____

For my senior year, I attended a Christian school in Upper Marlboro, MD. I was an outcast again. I had to learn new people, purchase new uniforms, and learn a new routine. While attending this school, I begin to explore my passion, dance. I created a proposal to make a dance group. Naturally, I would become the group's leader along with my friend, Jordan (not her real name), but someone from administration needed to supervise. The lady whom the school chose as our adult supervisor was Mrs. Parker (not her real name). Instantly, our personalities clashed. Mrs. Parker thought she knew everything. In my opinion, she really couldn't dance. Instinctively, she knew I didn't like the color of my skin. Although I had disdain for her dancing, she mentored me. Mrs. Parker shared with me her journey. She talked about growing up and feeling really ugly. She gave me compliments. She told me I was beautiful. She encouraged me to embrace my color. She assured me that nothing was wrong with my black skin. She told me that I was a rare form of beauty. In that moment, I felt encouraged! It's crazy how the people you don't like can impact your life. At that moment, she knew exactly what I was feeling. Her encouragement was important to me at that age.

As I previously mentioned, I started hanging out with someone out of curiosity not for a real friendship. I believe some of my teenage years were ruined because of LaTarsha (not her real name). Trying to be like someone else can take you down a dangerous path. Because of my poor self-esteem, I found myself in some very dark places. I took on her problems. I became drained emotionally and physically. Later, I began to dislike myself, which lead me to contemplate suicide. The battle in my mind was intense until I was 26 years old. Then, God spoke to me. He said, "Jocelynn, no one can be you but you. Have the freedom to be you." This statement meant that no one in this world could be me except me. There's only one Jocelynn Michelle Matthews.

Reflection Question: What are things you like about YOU that no one else can say or do because they aren't you? What makes you uniquely YOU? Write it down.

____

____

____

____

____

____

____

____

____

____

My College Years -The Pretty Years

Thirteenth grade came at a community college. Finally, people started telling me I was pretty, beautiful or cute. Many people would say, "OMG you are so pretty to be dark skin. Or, OMG I've never seen such a beautiful dark skin girl." While dating in college, my boyfriends would say, "You an exception, boo. I typically only date light skin girls." During my second semester of college, I was a little boy crazy (SMH). Any person that showed me attention and made me feel good, I hung out with them. College life became very challenging for me as a girl who grew up as a Christian. To continue fitting in, I started doing things such as missing class, smoking weed, drinking alcohol, fighting, playing cards and so on. Those choices were not smart, because, I wasted my own money. You see. My parents made me pay for classes.

The Experience

Life was quickly changing. My parents divorced. My mom was my best friend. She was leaving our home. My world crumbled badly. Somehow, the divorce drew my dad and me into a really close relationship. He started to tell me I was beautiful on a daily basis. Obviously, I started to believe it. I was hearing this from others. Now, my dad was saying it. I am beautiful. This statement must be true. Then, an experience happened with God. He said, "Jocelynn, someone once told this little girl she would never be anything because she was ugly and weak. Weakness was something she dealt with the majority of her life. She was weak when it came to men, women, friends, food, drugs, liquor, and just about anything. Whatever someone told her to do, she did. Wherever someone told her to go, she went. In life, she had no backbone and in her mind, that would never change. One day, at the age of 26, this woman had an experience that no one ever saw coming. The enemy had her so tied up that she reached her limit. She was fed up. You see. She got to the point where all she had was her weakness and God. One day she was crying about her frustrations. Randomly, she encountered a hug and a kiss that she never felt before, but not from a human." Yeah, I know you are wondering if not a human, then how? Well, there are angels that God can dispatch. God said, "That's what she encountered. God sent this woman an angel to show her His love. Love she never felt before. In that moment, he wiped away all the tears that she cried for years." The angel had a message from God. The angel said, "Daughter, when you are weak I am strong. Find your strength where I am. In me, you will find peace. In me, you will find love. In me, you will find joy. Come. Walk with me. The more you walk the more strength you will gain. I am strength." That little girl was Jocelynn! That's when my life changed!

Reflection Question: Is there an encounter that you have ever experienced with God and it changed your life completely like this one? Remind yourself of it.

____

____

____

____

____

____

Freedom Reigns

Guilt, fear, anger, insecurities, shyness and loneliness no longer reside in our lives. The enemy does everything he can to kill, steal and destroy us from the purpose and calling of God. We have to learn and know without any doubt that none of these things truly exist. Why? Jesus died for us over 2000 years ago. Why? He loves us. He thinks we are to die for. Why? The answers are endless. He sees us as righteousness. Today, allow Him to reconstruct the weak areas of your life. Allow your heart, spirit and soul to be open to receive from Him.

What do you need to be free from? In what areas of self-love or self-worth do you need to give over to Him? Today is the day. Jesus died for us so we can be free. Let's be completely free in Him. Jesus thought we were worth it all. When you know God, you know the truth. Living in His truth will bring freedom. Freedom is exactly what happened for me. In 2015, I cut all my hair off. I gained a self-love that was simply amazing. I gained a confidence that only God can give. It's not a cocky spirit but a self-loving spirit. God showed me to whom I belong.

Today, Jocelynn Matthews is this free-spirited powerhouse who finally stopped caring about what people thought. She loves her silky, smooth, milk chocolate skin. She embraces the weirdness about her that people didn't understand. She loves her chinky eyes and tiny little nose and much more! Jocelynn teaches others about self-love. She literally makes people stand in front of the mirror, say something they love about themselves, and when they can't do it, she tells them of where she has been. Jocelynn has a bubbly personality that can be a little over the top at times. She has a caring heart. She is a mover through dance. Currently, she goes back and forth with her weight because, simply put, she loves food-lol. That's something she can control. Jocelynn will never go back to a dark place of lack of self-worth. She is free to be completely who God called her to be!

Reflection Question: What has God freed you from while reading this chapter?

____

____

____

____

____

Promise To Self

Don't trip when these things or thoughts come back up, for today is our FREEDOM day. When these things do try to come back up, you remind the enemy of his place which is under your feet. Say this out loud in those moments, "So if the son sets you free, you will be really free." ~John 8:36 (NETB)

Fill in the blanks. *Today on, ______________________________, I am FREE to be ____ and I am walking in the FREEDOM from ____.*

Devotions

Has anyone ever said hurtful or mean things to you?

For all of my life, I have been called weird!!! When people referred to me as being weird, I thought it meant something negative about my image and myself. I would cry. Honestly, I felt insulted. As a result, I had low self-esteem. Yeah. I know. Some of y'all saying, "How could Jocelynn have low self-esteem?" Yes, honey. I did. You don't believe me? Ask either of my parents.

Because I perceived being called weird as something negative, my self-esteem remained low for many years. My peers called me weird as well as the grown ups. I couldn't figure out why kids or grown ups use the word. Instead, I assumed. Then, I believed. As a result, I saw myself as others labeled me. Subsequently, I began this journey of defining my weirdness. I am weird because my skin is dark. I am weird because I am a pk (preacher's kid). I am loud. Therefore, I am weird. I say yes, ma'am and yes, sir. I follow the rules. I am a dancer. I think I have nappy hair. So, I must be weird. I dye my hair different colors. I wear glasses. The thoughts were endless in my mind for a while.

Needless to say, I carried the thought of I am weird until I was 25 years old. Then, something happened. I was in a different headspace in my life. I had just joined a new church and my perspective changed. I was finally embracing life the way I should have a long time ago. As I grew spiritually, I realized that being weird was an AMAZING difference, not a criticism used to portray me negatively.

Spiritually, I learned that weird was good. As I matured, I began to see weird as a compliment. Weird meant to me at that moment that I was different, odd, fearless, imperfect, creative, dope, unusual, interesting, and peculiar. Above all, GOD spoke to me and said, "Jocelynn, you are weird. You are a chosen generation, a royal priesthood, and a holy nation." Feeling inspired, I tattooed on my inner arm the words Stay Weird. Uhm-huh. This tattoo became a subtle reminder to embrace all of my weirdness, because, it is how GOD created me.

If anyone is reading this and you are feeling low, remember, me saying this with my loud voice and my dancing hips! THERE IS NOTHING WRONG WITH YOU! Embrace your weirdness. Don't let anyone from this day forward make you feel bad about being different. Admit to yourself that you are different and live in your truth.

I promise. Life will be much easier. You will no longer be affected by what people say about you, how they think about you, or what they say to you. You will feel completely GOOD about life. Why? The answer is simple. I say, "No one can be you but you. Have the freedom to be you."

~ Jocelynn Matthews

Daily Devotion Scriptures

"I will give thanks to you, for I am fearfully and wonderfully made; Wonderful are your works, and my soul knows it very well."- Psalm 139:14 (NASB)

"But you are God's chosen treasure - priests who are kings, a spiritual "nation" set apart as God's devoted ones. He called you out of darkness to experience his marvelous light, and now he claims you as his very own. He did this so that you would broadcast his glorious wonders throughout the world." - 1 Peter 2:9 (TPT)

"God is within her, she will not fall; God will help her at break of day." - Psalm 46:5 (NIV)

Prayer

Dear Heavenly Father,

We come to now first of all thanking you for giving us life and uniquely creating us. Father thank you for all our flaws and imperfections. Help us embrace them and see the beauty of who we are individually because you see past all of that. You made us the way you desired us to be. You know the number of hairs on our heads, every thought, every emotion. Lord, forgive us for trying to be others, when you called us by our name. We repent and ask for a brand new heart. We thank you that we are brand new in you, we take on the mindset of Christ, we command our soul to line up with our Spirit man. Lord thank you for sending your son, Jesus Christ to die for us. We ask that you wash and cleanse us of our sins. Anytime the enemy tries to come and remind of us of our failures or lack of self-worth, self-love, we pray that we will remind him of his position which is under our feet. God ,we thank you for loving us. In the name of Jesus.

Amen.

BIO

Jocelynn Michelle Matthews

Choreographer, Artistic Dancer, Dance Instructor, Creative Director and Inspirational Coach

www.jocelynnmatthews.com

Jocelynn is a dancer, choreographer, and author. She has a dance background in Ballet, Jazz, modern, Hip-Hop, Lyrical, Liturgical, Afro Jazz, Contemporary, and African styles of dancing. She began her early dance training in Bowie, MD at the age of four years old. She is a high school graduate of Clinton Christian School where she established the first Clinton Christian School Dance Club. She is driven by God to be a mover and shaker, to transform and change atmospheres through movement, and to be powerful in her dancing and teaching. She believes that her destiny is to impress upon others to live FREE and walk in total liberty and newness of life. She has been embracing her gift in dancing for twenty-five years and choreographing for twelve years.

4

"THE CALL: BREAK UP YOUR FALLOW GROUND"

Cherelle Jeudy

Deep, twisted roots of bitterness threatened the beautiful garden that God planted within me. Years of dealing with abandonment and rejection allowed these roots to grow and, for years, endangered my purpose in life. Years of limiting beliefs about myself have resulted in failures, depression, and even thoughts of suicide. But God!

He rescued me from a potentially bitter end. Has my life's garden been saved forever? These roots are tricky. What I thought was gone was only dormant, waiting for the right moment to spring forth again. Life's disappointments began to water these roots, allowing them to creep up once again and threaten my purpose in life.

After years of struggling with a low sense of self-worth, in a moment when my life was completely quiet, I heard Him call, ***"Cherelle, break up your fallow ground. Your heart is hard and too full of the bitterness of life's disappointments. That is hindering you from fulfilling the purpose I placed in you."*** Desperate to be free, I allowed myself to go through the process to finally be released from the ugly, parasitic grasp of bitterness and walk in my God-designed destiny. And today, I want to share that process with you because you are reading this for a reason. You may be in your own battle with bitterness, and now is your time to break free.

A Field Considered

The rich farmer along with his hired man stood on the edge of an empty field. He smiled in deep satisfaction. He stood for a long while contemplating his plans and let out a great sigh.

"It's perfect. I am going to plant a bountiful garden. This garden will feed many."

The hired man looked up at the farmer thoroughly confused. He looked at the dry, cracked earth. It didn't look like rain touched this land in years. This field surely wouldn't be able to produce the results the farmer thinks. However, he stayed quiet and watched the farmer bend over and taste the earth.

The farmer nodded again, "I'm right. This field will require some work, but in time, it will produce the garden I desire."

I was once a daddy's girl. He was the center of my world for seven wonderful years. The man that I knew as daddy was god-like in my eyes, a superhero. He was strong, handsome, talented, ambitious, and he showered me with love and affection. I remember, he would sit me on his knee and speak life into me. Listening to him, I felt powerful, pretty, and most of all, loved. I was a mini superhero in training.

Suddenly, my castle of sand began to crumble. He and my mom got a divorce! One day, we were a happy family, and the next he was gone. Just like that. The news of their divorce barely made it to my heart before my mom delivered another devastating blow. This man was not my real father. When she told me this, something shifted in me. If I was not his daughter, then who was I?

Oh, but the mask! Most of us are familiar with THE mask, right? I learned early how to put it on. I learned how to smile when I was sad and laugh when I wanted to scream in angry frustration. There wasn't much tolerance for emotional outbursts in our home so I learned early that displaying these feelings served no purpose.

When I first met the man who would become my mom's second husband, I thought he was just a salesman passing through. However, he continued to come around to see my mom. Before I knew it, he was spending the night, and then he moved in. He had a lot of rules, and if we broke those rules, there were physical consequences. Other than that, he said very little to me or my brother; he barely acknowledged our existence. After they were married, my mom insisted that we call him daddy.

Wait. What?!? Why?!?

First, I already had a daddy even if he wasn't around anymore. Second, he didn't act like a daddy. It just didn't feel right. But, because my mom told me to, I obeyed. My stepfather and my mom would argue loudly and violently. There was nothing I could do. I became scared of him and didn't dare speak up or come to my mom's defense.

One night, I heard him tell my mother, "Your ex-husband called looking for the kids." I didn't hear my mom's response…I couldn't. I was too excited. My daddy called looking for me. Surely, he is going to call and tell us he loves and misses us. I probably waited three months before I realized he wasn't calling. Eventually, I concluded, "I have no daddy."

One time, they argued about us. My mom asked him why he didn't do things with my brother and me and why didn't he really talk to us.

In a moment of emotion, she asked, "Don't you love them?!?"

And he answered angrily, as he pointed his hands in my direction, "Of course I don't love them! They aren't my kids!!"

I sat on the couch as I tried to pretend that his words didn't just pierce my soul. My mother began to cry. Her efforts of recreating the family she had before failed. This man would not take my daddy's place. I realized then that a part of me still hoped that he would affirm me, and validate my worth; and it became apparent that he would never do that.

The Field Being Prepared for Planting

As the rich farmer surveyed the land, his hired man took a good look at the field as well. There was some potential for this field to produce abundant crops. Tired of seeing the prosperity of the farmer and being left with just his wages, he decided to take the field for himself. Once he figured out how to take this field, he would use this tactic to take more. The farmer had plenty of land, as far as the eyes could see. On every side of them, the land belonged to the farmer. Surely, he could spare some of his land.

Something crossed the eyes of the farmer when their eyes met. It rattled the hired man to his core. He looked down at the ground hoping his thoughts were not given away. The farmer gazed at the field, and said, "It is time to break this hard ground."

We were in the Hospital of the University of Pennsylvania. My grandma, the strongest woman I knew, was in the hospital sick. "Stroke," they said. She was conscious, but she was unable to talk. She was looking around the room in total confusion. Her guards were up as if she was in a room surrounded by strangers and not her family.

My rock, the woman I leaned on many days to share my heart with, looked at me as if I was a stranger. What was I supposed to do? I looked at my mom. Maybe, she would tell me that grandma would be okay. But, she looked as worried as I felt.

My grandma was a constant presence in my life. When my daddy's voice became silent, she spoke life over me. My grandma prayed for me. She took me to church every Sunday and told me about Jesus and how much He loved me. My grandma was the apple of my eye. To see her bedridden and unable to communicate was tough.

My grandma being a woman of faith, I thought she would appreciate if I prayed for her. I didn't know if God would listen, but I tried praying anyway. I was even specific on the timeline when I wanted her healing to take place. I asked God to completely heal her by my 15th birthday, which was two months away.

Shortly after I started praying, my grandma started to speak again. My mom and family brought her Bible and devotionals to help rebuild her language skills. And this time, when I walked in the room, her face lit up; and she looked at me with so much love. She never looked at me like that before, as if I were her favorite person in the world. I was thankful because God answered my prayers. But then, she had another stroke, and her health quickly deteriorated. I prayed that He would give me more time with her. However, a week after my 15th birthday, my grandma took her last breath.

Suddenly, the world around me felt unstable like quicksand since she was the rock that I stood on to keep me steady. And now, she was gone. I became very upset with God though I didn't want to admit it in my heart. What was the point of praying if He was going to ignore what I asked for?

That Stony Place

The hired man had staff under him and assured the rich farmer that he would make sure that the field would be properly tilled and ready for planting in early Spring. He called his workers and gave them specific instructions: "Till the land, but do not remove the stones."

They looked at him, confused for a moment, but remained quiet. The hired man could be a hard man, and his workers knew he would fire them without blinking an eye. Most of them knew the procedure and knew the hire man would blame THEM to keep his job. He had done this before. However, they worked obediently. The hired man nodded in deep satisfaction. He knew that, by this time next year, this land would be his.

After my grandma died, I felt completely lost. My grades dropped. My focus was no longer on school. It was on chasing love. We immediately went back to our routine while trying to ignore the gaping hole my grandmother left. My mom was busy working and finding her own happiness. So, I started looking for attention from boys. At first, it was innocent puppy love, but then I started getting attention from guys who wanted more than just a hug and kiss.

The boy who lived in the apartment downstairs said nice things to me. I paid a very high price to hear those words: I gave him my virginity at 15 years old. I eventually found out he was repeating those flattering words to another girl so I broke up with him. He called me every name in the book before getting on his knees to beg me to take him back, but I did not go back to him.

Around this time, my mom was hanging out a lot. So, it wasn't long before the neighborhood boys started hanging at my parent-free, cable-ready apartment. What I thought was clean innocent fun was far from innocent. A lot of those boys were going around telling the other neighborhood kids that they had sex with me, which was not true. I had a reputation without earning it. My attempt at finding love backfired.

I was so depressed and distraught over that. I started to sleep around. In my young mind, I figured if I had the reputation, I should earn it. Then, I got pregnant. I was 16 years old and had gotten pregnant by one of those neighborhood boys. I lost the baby early in my pregnancy before my mom even noticed. Losing the baby, the constant knocks by neighborhood boys, the loss of my daddy and my grandmother, and the absence of my mother left me feeling as if I were drifting. I had enough! I was tired of feeling sad, angry, and unloved. But God!

My best friend invited me to her house one weekend. Spending the night at her house on the weekends meant going to church. After the sermon, the pastor asked if anyone wanted to be baptized. I didn't plan on getting up. But I felt this tug on my heart, and before I thought twice, I got up to be baptized.

This changed me. I felt clean for the first time in a long time; I wanted to protect my new life in Christ. I cut all the boys out of my life. I stopped answering the door when they knocked and stopped answering the phone when they called. Shortly after, my mom announced that we were moving. Thank God for fresh starts!

I still had emotional baggage though. The storm within me was gaining strength, and I could hold the winds back no more. One day after school, I was talking to my best friend on the phone, and I just start crying uncontrollably. All the hurt and pain I felt just came out. My mom rushed home from work to comfort me and asked if I needed to see a therapist. I shook my head. She asked me again what I needed. I thought about the mystery person in my head.

I looked up at her and asked, "Who's my real father?"

After a long while, she said his name. I was upset, but I swallowed my feelings. When I met my dad, face to face, I saw him with new eyes. I'd met him before, but as my mom's friend in the military, not as my dad. I was so nervous. I don't think I said much. We had a polite conversation. He mentioned how much I favored my older sister and gave me her information so we could write. I didn't see him again for another year. This fed my insecurities. I really hated myself. ***Why couldn't I be prettier?*** I was upset but quickly swallowed it down — again.

I left for college shortly after our meeting, ready to blaze trails of success, kick butt and take names. I was going to make everyone who left wish they were a part of my life. That is, until I settled into school. Before my mom left my dorm room, self-doubt quickly set in. My inner voice started laughing at me, ***"What are you doing here? You don't have what it takes. You are changing your major again? What is wrong with you?"***

And I listened too. I came into freshman year, an honor student, ready to take on the world; and, by my sophomore year, I lost my scholarship. I didn't feel like I had what it took to be successful. I kept my mask intact. I played happy, always smiling, always laughing; but inside, that voice vexed me. I was stuck in self-doubt.

Then, I met someone who took my breath away. Up to this point, I was pretty sure that I would make it through college without being in a relationship. I had crushes, but they were distant and never developed into anything. After my baptism, I took a vow of purity. I was very protective of my second chance and decided that I wouldn't have sex with anyone until we were in a serious, committed relationship. I carried that mindset to school, which came in handy because it excluded a lot of people.

He was different and for the first time ,I opened myself to the possibility of love. In one breath I was prepared to profess my undying love, in the very same breath he broke up with me. And, to add salt to my wound, the voice within bellowed in arrogant laughter, ***"Girl, what were you thinking? What man has ever loved you? You thought he was going to be different?"*** I continued to function on the outside. I felt myself communicating with other people, still smiling, still laughing, but I was operating on autopilot. The mask, I so carefully applied, began to crumble and nothing I tried could keep it on.

Then, the bad decisions came, one after another. I started drinking. I started having sex again. I felt myself spiraling out of control and knew, if I didn't get myself together fast, I wasn't going to survive. So, I made the decision to quit school and go home. I arrived broken, defeated, and hopeless. I sunk into a deep depression. I began to think that death would be the best option. I wrestled with thoughts of suicide when painful memories surfaced. To keep myself busy, I decided to finish my degree and find a job.

My friend invited me to church again. I desperately wanted to feel a connection with someone and thought I should try God since everyone else had let me down. As the minister preached his sermon, it felt as if he read pages from my life. It felt like God was speaking directly to me. At the end of the message, I went up for prayer, and God met me there. I felt the burden melt away. As the tears flowed, I felt His presence, comforting and healing me. I was finally free.

Weeds and Thorns

It was late Spring, and the rich farmer arrived to inspect the progress of his garden. He seeded the fields earlier in the season and had great expectations. Upon surveying the land, he let out a small gasp. The field was full of weeds and thorns. He knew that weeds and thorns were a normal part of farming, but this field was consumed with them, and the plants were suffocating. Where the weeds weren't prevalent, the plants were dried and shriveled. He called the hired man.

The hired man quickly defended his work and suggested that the land was cursed. He offered to take the field from the farmer to nurse it back to health and return it when it was ready for planting. The farmer nodded thoughtfully and bent over the field to inspect. It had been tilled and watered, but something was not right. He dug his hands deep in the earth, and immediately felt the cold, hard presence of a stone. He kept digging and digging. More stones.

The farmer realized that the wicked hired man tried to cheat him out of his field. He dismissed the hired man and his workers at once. He turned back to the field and spoke, "Don't you worry. You will produce the garden I desire."

The anger that I had successfully swallowed for years had erupted, and there was no way of stopping the flow. I was tired of trying. After that healing touch from the Lord, my life changed. After stumbling a bit in the beginning, I rededicated my body to God and made a vow to stay chaste. I got involved with various ministries at the church: the choir, the youth ministry, the young adult ministry, the outreach ministry, and even served dinners in the kitchen, a time or two. I stayed pleasant and didn't ruffle any feathers. I was like Martha in the Bible.

I told myself that I was doing it to be helpful, but deep down inside I knew the truth. I enjoyed the praise for being meek and humble, when my heart was really filled with pride. My mask was very refined now. I smiled all the time. I pretended that I was always happy, but, under it all, I was crying. I was still nursing old wounds that I thought I gave to God on that altar years ago. I was too ashamed to admit that I was a fraud, so the mask stayed on.

Then, life happened. One incident after another and, before I knew it, I had drifted away. I drifted away from my church family, but, most of all, I drifted away from God. I just couldn't keep the mask on anymore. I was in a tumultuous season. The clouds were dark and threatening. The winds and the rains would not cease, and they ripped that phony mask off. I was completely exposed, and I did not like what I saw.

I became so angry that I stopped talking to God for a moment, even though I tried to tell myself that I wasn't angry at Him. I stopped reading my Bible. I tried to forge my own path to happiness because God obviously was not answering my prayers. But He will get your attention, won't He?

My frustration got the best of me one day, "Where did You go Lord? How come I don't feel You anymore? After all I did! Serving you without complaining. I was faithful to You, and You just let all of this happen to me? I have nothing. My family is struggling with no end in sight. And You are just sitting there not helping us out!"

And then, this scripture came to my heart, **"I will never leave you nor forsake you."**

"But God, all my life I've felt like no one truly loved me. Am I that unlovable?" **"I love you, Cherelle."**

"But, I'm alone God. Church was my whole life for nine years, and it seems like the only time people really showed that they cared was when I was working in the church. When I left, they forgot about me."

I heard this clear as day, **"Why did you go to church? For them or for me?"**

I shut my mouth immediately because I knew the answer. I stopped going to church for God. I don't know when that happened, but it became more about feeling validated, feeling important to people and not to God. I had no rebuttal. I had to go through all of that - all that loneliness, all that anger, and all that bitterness to realize that I was still chasing love - even in the church. I was banking that my relationship with people would make me feel valuable and loved instead of developing a relationship with Love. I knew I had to change.

Break Up Your Fallow Ground

The rich farmer called his workers to the field. They looked around amazed at its condition. One worker spoke up boldly and asked, "Sir, this

field is in bad shape. Will it be ready for the harvest this year?"

The farmer shook his head sadly, "No, this field will not be ready for this upcoming harvest."

The worker's disappointed expression mirrored the farmer's own. The farmer bent over and tasted the soil again. His eyes grew wide with excitement and, a broad smile crossed his face, "Ha! Do not fret my friend. The wicked hired man did not realize that his attempt to sabotage this land gave it the exact nutrients it was missing. After we remove the weeds, thorns, and the stones this land will be ready for the next planting. Come, gather the rest of the workers. Let's break up this fallow ground."

The news hit me, like a ton of bricks, when he said, "Cherelle, your mom has passed away." I thought I heard him incorrectly and asked if he was sure. "I'm waiting for the coroner to come and pronounce her. Call your brother and sister." And my mom's best friend/husband hung up. The world outside my window was bursting with life. Summer was in full bloom, but my world started to fade away.

I always loved my mom, but I can now admit that I was mad at her. For years, I was angry at her for divorcing my daddy, marrying an abuser, and then keeping my biological father a secret. For years, I felt like she didn't truly love me. However, I remained dutiful; I remained respectful. So, I wore the mask and pretended that everything was fine - when it wasn't.

Then, my mom got sick. She was hospitalized while in Philadelphia for a funeral. They stabilized her, and I thought she would be fine as long as she took care of herself. My mom went back to work for a while, but she kept getting sick and kept being hospitalized. This forced her to retire. My mom was always full of life, and to see her struggling to stay healthy was very hard to watch. Her illness kept her from living life to the fullest.

It was during one bout of sickness that my mom called me crying. She wailed into the phone, "I'm so sorry Cherelle. I'm so sorry." And then, as if she were watching a recording of our life, she apologized for everything. She even apologized about my dad. That surprised me. She said that I should not be mad at him but place the blame on her. And she just cried until she couldn't cry anymore. I prayed and asked God to help me to forgive her. From that moment forward, I was determined to leave the past in the past. And we grew very close.

My mom struggled with her health for eight years, and then her body became too tired to fight. There are no words in the English language that can properly explain what it feels like to lose a parent. A part of me did not want to move forward after my mom left. The one comfort that got me through some hard moments was that in spite of all our ups and downs, when she left this Earth, she knew her children loved her, and we knew that she loved us.

As things began to settle and reality set in that my mom was gone, I went through a dark and lonely moment. I became very, very upset with God again. This was the one prayer I really wanted Him to say yes to. And He took her instead. Why didn't He answer my prayers?

A friend contacted me a year after my mom passed away and asked if I would like to join her prayer group. I am so glad that I joined because it changed my life. We prayed for almost a year, and I made my peace with God. The fire these women had for the Lord was contagious! I developed a hunger to know Him for myself.

I delved into my Bible more and was led to Matthew 13, where Jesus spoke of the sower seeding a field. I've read this scripture many times, but this time I applied this scripture to my own life. When I read how the seeds were sown on stony ground (hardened hearts) and among weeds and thorns (the cares of this world), it resonated with me.

Eventually, I went to Jeremiah 4:3 and Hosea 10:12, and the call became very clear: ***Cherelle, break up your fallow ground! It is time to break up your stony heart and allow your heart to become a heart of flesh.***

Good Ground

The rich farmer and his workers worked tirelessly through the rest of the year to prepare the field for planting. It was a lot of hard work. The roots from those weeds and thorns were very aggressive and deep. Some roots were strong and had to be excavated using special equipment. The entire field would have been consumed if they did not intervene. When the farmer was satisfied, he wiped his brow and raised his arms in celebration.

"It's finally ready," the farmer exclaimed, "and now we can plant the garden. This ground is good and will yield many crops."

One of the workers gazed at the rich, black soil and grew excited because

he didn't have to pull anymore weeds and thorns, but as if reading his thoughts, the farmer interjected, "Oh, the weeds and thorns will come back. It is part of farming, but never again will they consume this field."

He patted the worker on his shoulder, "Come. Time to sow seeds."

I learned a lot about myself and where I truly was in Christ. I was weak and feeble. I desperately needed to be like Mary, sitting at Jesus's feet and letting His Word heal, strengthen, and rebuild me. I had help getting in the state of self-doubt and a low sense of self-worth, but, ultimately, it was my responsibility to go to the source of healing. I have grown up a lot, and a great indication of my growth is my youngest son.

Early in my pregnancy, I felt that something was different. I wasn't sure if I would carry past my first trimester but thank God the first ultrasound showed that my baby was healthy and growing. I let my mind rest a bit. Then, the blood work results came back. The doctor said that there was a strong chance that my baby had Down Syndrome, and that I should consider terminating my pregnancy. In my heart, I knew there was no way I was getting rid of my baby.

When my son was born, I knew right away that he had Down Syndrome. His eyes gave it away. I pushed down the feelings of doubt and focused on taking care of him while thinking, ***"I am going to love him no matter what."*** That is until I got home, and it was quiet enough for me to think. The anxiety started to rest on me like a blanket. I questioned, ***"Why? What did I do that made him like this? How is this going to affect his life? Will he be smart? Will people stare at him and treat him differently? Lord, please don't let me mess up his life! This seems like too much to handle."*** I cried for a week straight thinking the worse. Then, life threw us another curveball.

One morning, I was trying to feed him, and he just started spitting up. It was green, and it came up forcefully, so I called the pediatrician. They examined him and sent him straight to the emergency room. They suspected a bowel blockage and transported him to Children's Hospital in Washington, DC. Seeing him being transported in the glass enclosed crib broke me. Down Syndrome was no longer my worry. Something serious was happening to my baby. ***"Lord, I need your help. Please help us get through this,"*** I prayed continuously.

He spent three weeks in NICU with the diagnosis of a chronic disease in his colon. The news knocked the wind out of me, but, instead of crawling in despair, I immediately contacted my prayer sisters who prayed for me when I was too weak to pray myself. I placed my son in God's capable hands. Even when the doctors came with more challenges, I nodded and just prayed scriptures over him. Maybe it was all the people we had praying for him, but I felt such peace even in the face of this diagnosis. Being in the hospital everyday with my son made me realize just how far God has brought me. In the past, I would be in a state of panic, despair, and even depression because my son has special needs. Instead of shaking my fist towards heaven, I am leaning on my Father for strength.

I knew part of my healing process included forgiving my past. I called my dad shortly after my mom's funeral. He was there at her memorial, and that really touched my heart so I thought maybe I was ready to build that bridge between my dad and myself. That call was the start of something incredible. I am so happy that we are in a better place today. Reconciling with my dad set off a chain reaction. I knew that it was time to let go of what hurt me in the past and heal, once and for all. It was time to forgive and finally be free to receive ALL that God has planned for me!

I was a dried and thirsty field. I was lost and didn't know my purpose or even if I had a purpose. But, now I know that He always had me in mind, even with my imperfect beginnings and all the stumbles and disappointments along the way. I know that God had, and still has, wonderful plans for my life. I understand that every experience has served a divine purpose. It took bad relationships and even the death of loved ones to bring me closer to where God planned.

I am now a field of rich, black soil ready to receive the blessed seeds God is planting within me. There will be rains, and thank God for it, because what garden can thrive without water? Will there be weeds and thorns? Of course. Whose life is free from trouble? I'm just glad I know the One who can help me cultivate my blessed life garden.

Devotion

The Call: Break Up Your Fallow Ground

"For thus says the LORD to the men of Judah and Jerusalem: "Break up your fallow ground, and sow not among thorns." Jeremiah 4:3

Bitterness is a thirsty root. It is an insatiable cancer. If it is not checked, bitterness will work tirelessly to consume its host. We will all face offense, disappointment, failure, loss, grief, and/or separation. These experiences are part of living this thing called life. However, we have to decide if we will allow it to consume our thoughts and emotions, or will we allow ourselves to go through the healing process.

What happens if you experience a situation that leaves you feeling bruised and hurt? How you allow yourself to process the hurt and whether you are willing to heal from it, will determine whether you are watering that root of bitterness. Watering the roots of bitterness may keep you from fulfilling all God intended in your life.

You are here for a very important reason. When the Lord breathed into your nostrils for the first time, He breathed purpose and He breathed destiny. The intention is there and will remain with you for the remainder of your life. But it is up to you if you will meet your destiny. Don't let bitterness consume you and rob you from what God intended for you.

Bitterness will harden your heart, and like hard, fallow ground, which cannot receive or cultivate seeds, a hardened heart will keep you from fulfilling your complete potential. So, if you are nursing a lingering hurt or a wound, it is time to let it heal. Ask God to help you forgive the offense, so you can break free from the bondage of bitterness.

Prayer

The Call: Break Up Your Fallow Ground – Prayer

Father God in the name of Jesus,

I thank you Lord, for the one reading this right now. I lift them up to you right now. Lord, they have a deep hurt, a deep wound that they have been carrying with them. A heavy burden that they needed to be lifted. Lord, pull the roots of bitterness from their lives. Show them how to forgive those who have offended them. Just as you commanded Job to pray for his friends in Job 42:10, the friends who treated him badly in his weakest moment, Lord may they pray for their enemies and even their loved ones who hurt them. Lord may they pray for those who have hurt them, and release that hurt to you, Lord. May they turn that pain over to you Lord and allow you to heal them from their pain. Lord, we thank you for their healing, Lord we thank you for their restoration, Lord we thank you for the willful obedience to forgive others as you have forgiven us. And we pray this prayer in Jesus name. Amen.

BIO

Cherelle Jeudy

Author, Essential Oils Educator, and Health Coach

Cherelle Jeudy is the wife of an awesome man and the mother of four, energetic boys, who add joy and fulfillment to her life. She loves being a family woman and relishes in the fact that her first ministry is at home. She loves being her boys' first teacher, as she currently homeschools her three eldest sons. She also basks in being the caregiver of her youngest son, who the Lord blessed with one extra chromosome.

When she isn't serving her family, Cherelle is an author, an essential oils educator, and the founder of Happi Life Integrative Health Coaching where she helps her clients remove emotional, mental, and/or physical roadblocks that hinder them from achieving their health and wellness goals.

As an author, she uses her voice to implement healing from past hurts and trauma as well as encouragement to find joy in life regardless of current challenges. She believes that everyone has the capacity to be happy in life and hopes that through writing she can help people realize this.

As an essential oils educator, Cherelle helps her students understand that by utilizing God-designed ingredients and by cutting down on their use of chemical-laced products and incorporating natural solutions, they can give their body overwhelming support needed to thrive.

As a health coach, her approach does not dwell on calories, carbs, fats, and proteins. She does not to create lists of restrictions of good and bad foods. Instead, she collaborates with her clients to help them reach their health goals in areas such as achieving optimal weight, reducing food cravings, increasing sleep, properly managing their stress and maximizing energy in a way that is designed to be low stress, flexible, and rewarding.

Her prayer is that she will continue to utilize her voice to make a positive impact on the world around her.

5

"DANCE THROUGH LIFE ONE STEP AT A TIME…" **Brittney King**

Step One: Warm Up: *Inhale & Exhale*

A young girl with black hair, smooth melanin skin, exotic brown eyes, nice full lips, and a beautiful smile. You would think she had it all together but behind the makeup, hair,, and clothes a beautiful black girl is pretending to be fine while living in the silence of her feelings to make everyone else around her comfortable. This is what depression looks like. This girl was me. With tears rolling down my face as a teenage girl sitting in my room alone. Many nights my heart was heavy. As we did not share our feelings in this family and always brushed things under the rug and kept it moving, I couldn't turn off the negative thoughts running through my head. Why was I born to a single mother? Why was I dark skinned with the bad hair? Why did I feel a sad dark cloud over me? I had all these questions of 'Why me'. I felt alone, unhappy, sad, lost, ashamed and ugly. Looking for a sense of relief. Heart racing and palms sweaty. One late night, I pressed a hot iron against my thigh causing self- harm to numb the pain I was feeling. As I felt the burning sensation run down my leg, I began to focus on that pain hoping to feel better. Did I start to feel better you may wonder? The answer is No! While it gave me temporary control of my environment on the outside, my negative thoughts remained inside.

Looking at myself in the mirror. I started to feel ashamed as I couldn't believe what I did to my own flesh and blood. I knew then, I could not live in this darkness any longer. I didn't want to hurt myself anymore and began to pray to God for help and forgiveness. It was time for me to help myself and go back to what I knew. Dancing. It filled my heart and gave me peace. Having been trained in different styles of dance since the age of three. Dancing was always my escape from the real world. It created an atmosphere where I could express myself without talking. Dance let me be free in my own skin, to embrace my body as I move freely. I thank God and my mother for giving me the gift of dance. It pulled me through some tough times in my life. My mother had her challenges with paying for my dance classes but she continued to work hard to make ends meet. As dance was the one thing I loved the most and as I like to say, saved my life. My mother always had faith in God that I'll continue dancing. She always taught me to lean on his holy word for guidance for he is our provider. If you are feeling down, without hope, overwhelmed, the bible can lift your spirits and give you a fresh view on life! Here's a bible verse for you!

John 14: 27

Peace I leave with you; my peace I give you. I do not give to you as the world gives. Do not let your hearts be troubled and do not be afraid.

Step Two: Ballet: *Express*

During high school living in the south I worked part-time jobs to help my mother. When I had extra money, I helped with my extra activities for dance and pageants. I would like to enter pageants as I enjoyed performing through dance any chance I got, dressing up in a gown, wearing my hair weave and putting on makeup. It made me feel pretty. Although, I would never win the crown, but came close from time to time for runner up or placed in the top 3. It was always a Caucasian girl or a light skinned girl to win the title. I felt like lighter was better. Also, being the minority in my dance classes growing up, I was always put in the back rows, and this affected my self-esteem, but I kept on dancing anyway as no one could take my gift away. Family reminded me that I was beautiful, although I didn't feel that way about myself. I was not loving the skin I was in, which took me to a place of darkness. But I realize, I was looking for acceptance through people when I needed to love myself without the glitz and the glamour. When all along I already had a crown given to me by God.

As a girl, I dreamed of the family I would see on television and the lifestyle I thought others had. With two loving parents in a home of laughter, spending time together, having fun and working through challenges together as a unit. Carrying that resentment in my heart for not having my father around added to my self-hatred. I was feeling abandoned with my mother playing the role of mom and dad. Therefore, I continued hiding my depression from my family and friends.

I wanted my dad to build a life with my mother so we all could be happy together and wouldn't have to struggle alone. As my dad always showed my mom respect in front of me. I thought having them together would be great for me. But as you get older you realize fairytales are fiction and what's behind closed doors, is not always what it seems. As I think back, I wouldn't change my upbringing as it helped me learn how to survive and be resilient. Writing a letter to my dad was the best way to help me heal from my daddy issues. Although I never sent the letter to him. It was freeing! As I wrote my feelings down, I began to cry as I was letting go of the feelings I never shared. It was time to free myself of hurt and to forgive my father. I didn't recognize I was still holding on to hurt from years ago. I advise you to write a letter to someone you need to forgive.

Writing Activity: Get a journal and write your forgiveness letter:

____

____

____

____

____

____

____

____

____

____

____

____

Scriptures to help forgive the past

Ephesians 4:32

Be Kind to one another and tenderhearted. Forgiving one another as God forgives you.

Colossians 3:13

Bearing with one another, and if one has a complaint against another, forgiving each other, as the Lord has forgiving each other, as the Lord has forgiven you. You must forgive.

A poem for you….

A Flower that Grows in Darkness

When my seeds were planted, I first grew from the roots

Even in darkness, my roots took its place in the soil. Like my soul,
a small plant beginning to emerge,
breaking through the darkness this flower begins to bloom

All flowers eventually need sunlight

As flowers need to be watered and nurtured even in the dark soil,
our dark soul can grow into that flower
as it depends on our environment and the company we keep

We must use our gardening skills well

As a flower can grow from darkness,
while there is so many reasons why is shouldn't exist

That flower must be celebrated

That flower maybe you

Like a flower, new seeds will grow inside that flower,
like new day, new hope and a new grace

As the soil, my soul will grow into the sunlight
as I feel the warm air touch my petals

I know I am here,
I'm alive like a flower and I have blossomed out of the darkness

Step Three: *Hip Hop. Be Strong*

A southern girl to the city lights. I had the opportunity to move to Washington, DC after college. Working a dead-end job at the hair store, living from house to house. I needed a new change of environment desperately. Excited for this new adventure, yet nervous on this new chapter in my life. As a recent graduate, it was hard finding a job at the time. While I was not being responsible with my money. Exploring this new city, partying and drinking. My savings were getting low. While letting my ego get the best of me, I did not want to be a burden to ask family for help. While I knew I couldn't ask my mother for money, as she didn't have any. I realize I was carrying on my mother's bad habits of money management. Her unhealthy relationship with her boyfriend, the pain of never knowing her birth mother, hiding her learning disability, feeling like the black sheep of the family, losing her car, home, and being homeless at one time. Seeing my mom broken weighed heavy on my heart as I wanted to help her but I couldn't help myself at the time. That triggered my depression but my mom couldn't see my depression, because she was dealing with her own. I started to feel more depressed; going down a dark path looking for pleasure in all the wrong places. As I still couldn't find a job since my new move. Times were rough and I lost it all and my way of transportation, my car. Desperately thinking of ways to make money. I got the idea to audition to be a stripper at a local club to make some money to pay my bills and to keep up with my lifestyle. Music pumping, dim lights, poles, alcohol, drugs. Everyone looking for a good thrill. There I was as the DJ announces, WELCOME TO THE STAGE CHARLOTTE! Yes, my stripper name was Charlotte, not sexy at all right but that's what I came up with. I had to convince myself that I could do this and I dreadfully needed the money. I couldn't resist the temptation of getting that fast money. That week felt like a rush, like a drug. Although, I knew deep down in my soul this was wrong and not of God, I still couldn't help but to test the waters. Shortly after praying to God to get me out of this club as this lifestyle was not for me, I found a new job. I prayed to my heavenly father thanking him for his grace and mercy as it came right on time. I asked for forgiveness and repented for my sins and my wicked ways. Thanks to the new job, I was able to afford dance classes too. I started to take local dance classes around the area to continue dancing in a more positive way. As dance always kept me sane and gave me strength.

2 Chronicles 7:14

**If my people, which are called by my name,
shall humble themselves, and pray, and seek my face,
and turn from their wicked ways;
then will I hear from heaven,
and will forgive their sin, and will heal their land.**

Step Four: ***Liturgical. Reflect & Release***

Breaking the Silence

As I dropped to my knees very Surprised! I was with a child, as I could not hold back my smile

It was our little secret, just you and mommy for a while

As time passed, we became more and more excited day by day, week by week

It became the hardest secret to keep

Daddy and I talked about you all the time

Who will you look like? What will we name you? Are you a boy or a girl? Can't wait for you to come into our world.

Feeling So happy and Alive!

The first day of our scan has arrived!

Finally, we get to see our little baby and hear the heart beat

Holding on tightly to your Daddy's hand

As I lie there on the bed,

the nurse begins to Shake her head

As she looks at me and said, I'm so sorry but we cannot find the heart beat!

I'm so sorry as she repeats

Everything in that moment stopped and

my heart begins to drop

As tears ran down my face

Me and your Daddy begin to embrace

We begin to pray and ask God from above to please bring our baby back,
for this child is wanted and loved

The life we had planned was now wiped out and now filled with doubt.

As we went back home you were gone even though you were still inside me

As I thought to myself, what did I do wrong?

For I'm not the same soul I used to be

For my heart continues to bleed

I asked God to fill me up in my time of need

As the physical pain and heartache sits upon me

God hears my cries and continue to bless me, for I am still Alive

I see God is in control and won't put more on me then I can bear

for he is loving and always cared

Although Life can be so unfair, As this untold story, I had to share

For I will never forget you

As I think about you from time to time

I'll hold a piece of you in my heart

For you were mine

What a great creation of God, now placed in the skies above,

For you are loved

And when I look into the night sky,

Let there be light

And may you be resting in peace among the stars shining so bright!

Till this day, I'm still healing from my pregnancy losses as it brings up sadness to my heart. It's like a nightmare that I cannot escape from. I recently had a second pregnancy loss and this time was a bit tougher as we had all these baby gifts and items all over the house after our gender reveal party. My husband and I for sure thought this baby was going to make it to term as God waited two years to bless us with another seed. I couldn't believe my water broke early at 5 months. I had a rupture of the membrane and all my amniotic fluid leaked out that the baby sits in. We were so devastated, I couldn't help but to blame myself. Here I am, 31 years old, physically fit through dancing, no previous health issues and I'm considered to be high-risk when it comes to pregnancy.

You never think tragedy will happen to you until it does. Then your true test of who you really are is at the surface and you will either evolve or sink. I delivered our baby boy, Nehemiah, on June 4th, 2018. I remember holding his beautiful little body as his face was filled with peace. After the loss of the baby, sex intimidated me as it reminded me of the baby. I hated looking at my stomach because my baby bump was gone. I had to allow myself to heal and not avoid my feelings. I had to understand that those feelings are natural during this traumatizing event. My son's name, Nehemiah, means comfort of God and I ask just for that. For God to send me comfort during this time. The memory of his peacefulness pierces into my soul as I will take my son spirit with me every day and live in peace. I come to learn, grieving takes time and is a process. One positive thing I can say, is that God still kept me alive and well. I have faith that God will give me another chance to have a baby, but he is trying to tell me something and whatever it is I need to make sure I am receiving it. I realized, life doesn't get easier, but we must continue dancing through life one step at a time. Finding your passion is one thing, following it is another. As I continue to heal, I use dance to help me cope with my heartache. We all have something that makes us feel alive, that adds a little extra meaning to life, an activity that gives us a sense of fulfillment and purpose. If you don't know what that might be (yet), choose the hobbies, your natural talent, careers and pastimes that excite you the most; because those are the things worth chasing! I thank God for letting me step out on faith and pursue my dreams of owning my own Dance company and he continues to prove to me that I can do this! Dance Therapy Arts brings me so much joy as it is also my baby. I will continue to work even harder to nurture my passion. For many days dance has been the one thing to save me from depression. I'm very blessed to have great support around me and to share my love of dance with beautiful girls and women who are amazing! They give me the fight to keep going! As this is only the beginning! Inhale, Exhale, Express, Be Strong, Reflect and Release as you Dance Through Life One Step at A Time

Break Free Forever

As I cry out to the Lord!

Help me to heal from my past and be present for my future

Father, please forgive me as I will forgive myself and others

Let your light shine as we surrender

Like Angels Wings

Protect us under your arms as

Our spiritual guides are near us

As God is within us

No longer should we live in bondage

For we have the courage to break free forever

We must help change our future as it approaches

With sacrifices being made

There may come pain

But with pain comes strength

As we must not live in vain

As God will guide us to our tribe

And we all will rise and march with pride

As one day our battle will be over and there will be no more cries

As we have broken free forever

Devotion

Sometimes you have to be broken for God to work in your life, for you to see who you were created to be. You have to accept the reality of the things that has happened to you. You cannot heal from what you do not face. Move forward from your past or it will hold you hostage. Be free from it and beautiful things will start to happen. Walk into your vision with confidence and don't look back. Free yourself of the past. Forgive yourself and others as God continues to gives us grace and mercy. See the continued blessings through your challenges. God has a training program as it's not about you, but God's work. For we are all God's children here to help others. When you give, you will receive. Living in guilt can hold you back from your healing. You must change your habits in order to change your life. Shift your thinking process and thoughts. Let God know he can trust you and he will bless you. Live in your truth and be patient with yourself as God can provide peace to accept things we cannot change. Let go of insecurities as it doesn't hold value and we must look fear straight in the eyes as it does not have power. Don't continue to live in the past for what's done is done. Take authority of your life as tomorrow is a new day to try again. Your plan will change as God uses you for his path. There are moments in life that come to test you and break you. But those tests can become breakthroughs. As the core of who you really are will map out your future.

Prayer

My heavenly creator, we humbly come to you with honor. We put our trust in you father as he who dwells in the shelter of the Most High will rest in the shadow of the Almighty. I asked you to cover us with your faithfulness and shield us under your everlasting arms. Heal our hearts father from pain, hurt, and sickness. Take care of our mind, body and spirit. Guide us on our path and help us to stay focus on your holy word. As we should not walk in fear as you live within us. Help us to be more like you God, to walk in our calling. To be the light in someone's life. I pray for good health for us all and to be free of any illnesses. Help us Lord in managing our finances and all areas in our lives, to spend less and enjoy life more. I ask that you lead us all to our purpose and to help one another along the way. Protect our family, friends, neighbors, country and those around the world. As there will always be challenges, I ask that you help us respond in a positive way. For us to live stress free. Bless those Father who are reading this and bless those we come in contact with. Bless us on our jobs, careers businesses, goals, aspirations, and dreams. Thank you, Father, for your everlasting love and grace. Continue to bless us as we walk with you every day.

BIO

Originally from South Carolina, currently residing in Washington, DC. Mrs. Brittney King was once a woman who lived in silence with depression. Although she faced many challenges. She is resilient and walks through life with blind faith. Mrs. King is a courageous entrepreneur and holds a Bachelor of Arts degree in Business Marketing, a Master of Arts degree in Teaching, and has over fifteen years of preparation and experience as a professional dancer. In preparation for her career as a dancer and teacher, she received training at the Freed Performing Arts Center (Sumter, SC), Broadway Dance Center (New York, NY), and South Carolina State University (Orangeburg, SC). Throughout her career, she has performed with a variety of celebrities in a number of shows and venues.

Mrs. King's love for the arts and her commitment to social relevance inspired her to develop Dance Therapy Arts (DTA) in 2016. DTA provides a dance program that connects King's training and experience with her desire to teach people of all ages to practice creative expression through dance and fitness. Ms. King currently teaches ballet, jazz, hip hop, contemporary, lyrical, West African, and liturgical at Dance Therapy Arts. She is also licensed to teach Zumba and has created a new form of body movement called "dance therapy arts fitness". Mrs. King connects the world through artistic excellence and social relevance by creating vibrant new works and serving the field of performing arts through teaching people of all ages from 3 to 70 years old. She focuses on the mind, body and soul while educating the community through the art of dance, experiencing the power of movement freely and meditation. Mrs. King mission is to promote positive change to happen in one's life through dance and mindfulness practice.

The future for Mrs. King and DTA is bright, as she prepares to expand her "touch" on the world and embody the words of Dele Olanubi "I wish to live a life that causes my souls to dance inside my body".

6

"IT HAD TO HAPPEN"
LaToya Johnson

My Life Changed Forever

I woke up to a beeping noise and a hissing sound. As I struggled to open my eyes, I was overwhelmed by the thick smell of band aides and chemicals. The smell was familiar to me but couldn't remember where it was from. I didn't know where I was. Even though my vision was blurry, I could tell that I was in a small room. I started panicking because I still didn't know where I was. All I knew is that I was in a small room, I could see that a curtain hanged to one side and the other side was glass. I could also see people in white jackets and the others in green uniform, in the hallway standing around an oval shape desk.

I tried to speak but I couldn't. I had a tube down my throat to help me breathe and IV in my arm. I was thinking what's going on? What happened? It dawned on me that I was in the hospital. Why I am in the hospital? What happened? I need to get up and figure out what's going on. I was determined to get up out this bed. It felt like someone was pouring gasoline on an already burning fire, down my throat as I was pulling the breathing tube out of my mouth. My throat was burning. I started coughing, trying to catch my breath. I was pissed at this time. I gained the strength like the Incredible Hulk, yanking the IV out and I tried to get out of the bed. The more I tried to get up, I wouldn't move. Before I could process why I couldn't move. The nurses and two doctor's rushed in my room. I could hear a female say, how did she pull the breathing tube and IV out? Before I could hear the answer or process it, I was thinking why did she say that? I felt a pinch & I was out. I spent five days in the ICU and I was out of the woods on Sunday May 13th, Mother's Day. I couldn't imagine what my mom was going through, having her only child in the hospital from a gunshot wound to the head.

Mother's, can you imagine your only child was shot in the head?

Welcome Home

After all of the commotion and excitement from my welcome home party. I appreciated the love and support from that day but with a brain injury it was too soon. With my brain injury I had to readjust to my surrendering environment. Even though this was my house it was new to me but it wasn't also.

Everyone was leaving or already left, I was exhausted and wanted to go to bed. Then I realized how I was going to get up the stairs. My Step Dad Sam wasn't strong enough to carry me. We had to call a family friend to come back to carry me up the stairs to my new room (the master bedroom). As I was being carried upstairs I had to lay my head on his chest to avoid bumping my head. Since the shooting my paranoia level was high and I don't trust this man. With me being tensed and scared, my brain and body didn't know how to react and full spasticity (Spasm) and tone kicked in my legs and in tremendous amount of pain.

-Spasticity (Spasms) this contraction causes stiffness or tightness of the muscles and can be very painful

Not only do I have to make sure I don't hit my head. I have to make sure my legs didn't hit the columns & rail going up the narrow staircase. I can't believe these are the same stairs I was running up and down 32 days ago. Now I had to be carried up them. He I tried to scoot up in the bed and I went to grab onto the rail on the side. That's when it hit me that I wasn't in the hospital bed anymore, I was home. As bad I wanted to go home, it was more challenging than anything I expected. I didn't even have the strength to pull myself up in the bed. My mom or Step Dad Sam, had to make sure that I was in a comfortable position in the bed. It was so embarrassing and humiliating. Most nights I would lay there crying and converse with myself because I was still mad at God and I refused to pray. (Not knowing when I am having a conversation with myself is praying).

Coloring would help me to stay calm & relieve my headaches. I suffer with all kind of migraines/ headaches since the age of 6 yrs. old. Some pain I learned tolerate but with this injury my hypersensitive levels were high.

When my Home Care Physical Therapy (PT) help me walk 10 steps. I had to strain to help slide through as my Home Care PT assisted me. It felt like I was doing most of the work because how hard I was straining, but it was all my PT. With each movement my migraine would get worse. It felt like my brain was oozing out of my ears. As I would start to cry my physical therapist would strongly encourage me to stop and sit. I refuse to stop. I was determined to continue to the end. After every PT session, I would have to lay down and cry but I couldn't cry as hard like I wanted to because I was scared that my brain was actually going to start oozing out of my ears.

I would lay in the bed with my frozen eye patch and a pillow. That is the worst migraine I ever experience. I was going to continue practice walking until it got easier. I believe it. I had a vision of me walking again and I wasn't going settle for nothing less than that.

I learned a lot about my body and muscles that I didn't realize. **Did you know with each step you take, your butt muscles are contracting in order for you to take one step?**

Mt. Vernon Rehabilitation Hospital

I was admitted to Mt. Vernon Rehabilitation Hospital on August 9th and discharge on September 9th. I was excited to get started with a rehabilitation because I refuse to accept this. I don't like this person that I have become.

My second day there, Nurse Betty ask me would I like to take a shower. My eye almost out his head. I haven't had a shower in three months. My obsessive-compulsive disorder (OCD) kicked in and she draped the shower benches she understood that I was recovering from a traumatic brain injury.

I don't trust this bench.. I'm very cautious about everything especially my health. I held the shower head above my head, allowing the water to come from the top of my head down my body and it felt like heaven. It's been exactly three months to the day since I took a shower. I was so excited I washed my body three times. I would have stayed in there longer, just to make up for lost time. After that shower I slept like a baby my second night there. You never know how much you are going to miss doing things you do on a daily basis like take a shower. Never take the smallest thing for granted.

While at Mt. Vernon Rehab Hospital, I had six days of intense Physical Therapy (PT) and five days of Occupational Therapy (OT), Speech Therapy and Recreational Therapy (RT).

Physical Therapy (PT): is care that aims to ease pain and help you function, move, and live better. Relieve pain. Improve movement or ability. Prevent or recover from a sports injury.

Occupational Therapy (OT): is a form of therapy for those recuperating from physical or mental illness that encourages rehabilitation through the performance of activities required in daily life.

Recreational Therapy (RT): also known as therapeutic recreation, is a systematic process that utilizes recreation and other activity-based.

Speech Therapy: is training to help people with speech and language problems to speak more clearly. Speech therapist also helped with reading, spelling, grammar and comprehension.

I still had my depression days, especially when my dyslexia came back five times worst. My dyslexia affects my reading ability, difficulty memorizing, difficulty spelling, difficulty understanding and of course headache. All the hard work I put in to overcome my learning disability was for nothing. Really God?

If I am having a migraine every day that I wake up, I have a damn migraine. What is the point of keep trying?

I just wanted to give up so many times. There was a Bible in the draw of my hospital tray. I started flipping through it and I stopped on the book of John. As I scrolled through my eyes landed on John chapter 10 verse 10. The words were in red that means Jesus is speaking. As I read his words instead of taking it as a positive I took it as a negative thing. I wasn't ready to accept my new life. This was too hard and with waking up every day with a migraine how was I ever going to do my exercise? How was I ever going to walk again?

There was a television a local show about Stop the Violence in our neighborhoods. There was a few go-go band members, rappers and community activist were on this show. They talked about ways to save our communities and people. That's when it dawned on me, I have a story that everyone needs to hear & see me. I'm a real miracle. My story hit a lot of different topics, Gun Violence, Drugs and Domestic Violence. My story will save lives and inspire people. My determination and desire kicked in but I didn't know where start?

At the end of my 30 days, I was released. I felt comfortable and a little more confident and adjusting to my new life. I could stand pivot and wearing under wears during the day. All of my therapist made sure that I had everything I needed. I had a wheelchair, a bedside commode and a shower chair before I was approved to go home, I would need a wheelchair ramp and that was done. I was on my way home and was excited to sleep in my own bed. I had Home Care Therapy sessions continued until I could got into the Outpatient sessions.

Unconfident Back to Confident and Closer God

Since the shooting I do not like the person whom I have become. I didn't recognize this person at all. I always gave 110% to everything that I do. I was confident in myself, my beauty, my ambition and my go getter spirit. I was a determined, professional, black woman who loved to have fun and party but was about my money.

I have found myself jealous at the people on television because they were walking, dancing or running. Jealous of people who had the ability to be free to leave out so freely. Jealous of females who looked fly from head to toe. Their hair looking good, outfit is fly and sexy, with a pair exotic stilettos. Looking like me before my shooting now I to settle for a squeaky walker and a pair of sneakers with two uncomfortable Ankle- Foot - Orthosis AFO leg braces. Every time I go somewhere, someone have to take my walker up and down the stairs. I have never had a jealous bone in my body. I knew all I had to do was work hard to achieve, those things that I desire.. I became very vulnerable and always sick, mad or depressed. My life has become very beige and boring instead of full excitement and fun. I felt mentally drain and so uninspired but refused to be a victim. I was lost and I didn't know who I was anymore. I needed someone to save me because I didn't have any positive males around me and God seem to not care. I allowed myself to be open and honest with someone who ended up crushing my heart into a million pieces. My heart was hurting so bad that I took a handful of pills to stop the pain but not to kill myself. This was my darkness hour and it was time to pray because I was mad with God. I forgave my ex because as a result of that situation brought me closer to God. I know God is the one, that's important. Nothing else matters..

Today Was a Good Day

I woke up and I laid there for a minute than I sat up for a minute to see how I was feeling. I shouted, "Thank you Heavenly Father for allowing me to see another pain free day. Thank you Father for the new possibilities and opportunities that this day has for me. Use me Lord as you see fit for me and that's living out your purpose over my life. With your guidance and direction my goals and dreams will coming into a reality. In Jesus name, Amen."

After being sick the entire month of October, I woke up with no excruciating migraine or feeling nauseous. I was thrilled and I jumped up full of gratefulness. I couldn't waste God's blessing. I decided to go to church instead of watching church on tv.

Church was great and the message motivated me. I wasn't ready to go home after church so I went to my friend 'Tamika's Tea party. I'm going to support my girl since I didn't get out much because I'm always sick.

She had a good turnout I didn't know what to expect definitely not the testimonies that I heard. I like what I heard about the tea but I was blown away when I heard the testimony of NutraBurst. One of the Directors said her sister had migranelypse. It is when you have a seizure followed up with a migraine. She had to quit her job and to go on disability. The Director said she gave her sister a month supply of Laso Tea and a bottle of NutraBurst. Within three weeks her sister noticed that she did not have as many migrainelypse. That sparked my interest since I had migraines since the age of 6 years old now I have this bullet in my head. Let me test these products out.

I heard another testimony about NRG aka Happy pills. It help my friend with her postponed depression. I most definitely need NRG in my life. I ordered the Laso Tea and NutraBurst, three weeks later is when I had my first migraine. I was amazed with these products. I suffered in agony pain for 8 years taking prescription medicine and dealing with their side effects. These all natural products as simple as Laso Detox Tea and NutraBurst liquid vitamins was able to keep me migraine free and nausea free for days and not hours or not at all. They are all natural products with no side effects was a "win, win". When I did start taking NRG, I noticed a big difference. I was **Unconfident Back to Confident and Closer God**

Since the shooting I do not like the person whom I have become. I didn't recognize this person at all. I always gave 110% to everything that I do. I was confident in myself, my beauty, my ambition and my go getter spirit. I was a determined, professional, black woman who loved to have fun and party but was about my money.

I have found myself jealous at the people on television because they were walking, dancing or running. Jealous of people who had the ability to be free to leave out so freely. Jealous of females who looked fly from head to toe. Their hair looking good, outfit is fly and sexy, with a pair exotic stilettos. Looking like me before my shooting now I to settle for a squeaky walker and a pair of sneakers with two uncomfortable Ankle- Foot - Orthosis AFO leg braces. Every time I go somewhere, someone have to take my walker up and down the stairs. I have never had a jealous bone in my body. I knew all I had to do was put in the hard work to achieve those things and more. I became very vulnerable and always sick, mad or depressed. My life has become very beige and boring instead of full excitement and fun. I felt mentally drain and so uninspired but refused to be a victim. I was lost and I didn't know who I was anymore. I needed someone to save me because I didn't have any positive males around me and God seem to not care. Sad, depressed and showing signs of procrastination NRG not only gave me energy it also worked as a blocker. It blocked the negative energy from consuming me and bring me down. They are truly my happy pills.

These products saved my life. I wasn't sick all the time. I can go to family function and other events instead of being accused of using my illness as an excuse. I started to think about if these product are helping me, I know they will help a lot of people.

Especially help others like me who have a brain injury. Brain injury survivors rarely have good days. Then there are people who are always looking to lose weight and improve their health. Since my injury has prevented me from getting a job this opportunity came right on time. I joined the Total Life Changes aka TLC.

My friend Tamika told me about how she won the title of number 1 female network marketer in the world, plus she is an African America aka Black woman. How she is very reliable and inspiring. Her name is Stormy Wellington. I watched some her videos on YouTube. Her hustle, drive and determination spirit, reminded me of the old me. This company, the leadership is what I needed. It is something that I definitely needed to grow, to heal and to learn. I was tired of being sick and tired all the time literally. So I decided to change my mindset to change my success, my wealth and my money.

Every morning I forget for a second about my disability until I turn over and my purple walker is there by my bed. On this particular day I woke up depressed and just tired.

The title of one of the WUAW call was: **It Had To Happen.** As I watched Coach Stormy on the Instagram speak on the topic hit me like a ton of bricks. It made me start to think about the different events that has happened in my life was a lesson.

From me having to fight every day in elementary for 3 years, girls who I thought was my friends. That taught me strength, courage and I can't be friends with everybody. Some people will be jealous of you no matter what.

At the age of 4 years old hiding in the trash can so the bad man can't hurt my

private area again. That taught me to be smart and to protect myself and to use my surroundings to my advantage. Being diagnosed with migraines at 6 years old and depression as a teenager. That lesson taught me to develop a high tolerance to pain and sadness.

Being raped twice, taught me to develop a resilient spirit and even as I was being raped I wasn't going to let him take my power away. I will not be a victim. I'm not going to let him or no one to take my power. I'm too strong to let him push me into a victim mentally. I am nobody's victim. I'm way too strong to become weak. My mama didn't raise no punk. The betrayal, disappointment, heartbreak, loneliness, being a survivor of domestic violence, and suicide attempts. All of these tests and challenge that I have overcame. He was preparing me for this season in my life to survive a gunshot wound to the head.

After I was over anger with God. I heard him talk to me clear one day in the shower saying. "I would survive whatever come your way just like I knew you would. I created you to be a survivor.

You have survived what have killed most people. You was the right person to be the example of hope, miracles and the strength to never give up. When you enter a room now they to see your struggles and your tendency of not giving up. If I can maneuver around and make it work so can others. You will give them strength. He also said, "I didn't do this to you but for someone else. Someone else who is not as strong enough, need to see you and hear your story. They need to see your fight and drive."

He built a platform out of my pain so I will be able to impact thousands to millions of people's lives. My life is a struggle every day but I refuse to be a victim but instead a Vic-tor. I am blessed and honored to be the 5 % of gunshot wound survivors and grateful to be 3% chosen to live an independent life.

As I started to sit back and think about were my life would be if I wasn't in this situation, I only saw two options. Option one, me in a prison jumpsuit with a drug conspiracy charges, serving 25 years. Option two, me laying in my purple casket with white trimming, dressed in purple. The casket was surrounded with white and purple flowers.

I have learned from the Wake up and Win calls, to speak life into myself and affirmations because nothing about my new life is easy. Every day is a struggle but I faith in God because he blocked the bullet from taking my life. He has a purpose for my life and I can't wait for the blessing. When I accept my situation and realize that all things are either caused by him or allowed by him for his own purpose and through his perfect will and timing. There will always be negative people and things happen that's hard but I will never give up. I will never give the devil or my haters the satisfaction.

I am ambitious, persistent and faithful woman. I am determined not to let my situation defeat me. If I didn't let my circumstances defeat me and this was only a chapter of my life. Never take life for granted not even the smallest things in life. Celebrate everything, nothing is too smaller. Be aware of the company because not everyone has your best intentions. Always trust and believe that God is with you at all times. As long as you have breathe in your body, anything is possible. You just have to Believe & have Faith.

BIO

LaToya Sharee Johnson is an international author, speaker, and entrepreneur. With an impactful message that will save lives around the world. LaToya's life changed on May 8, 2007, when she was shot in the head. Eleven years later she has been defying the odds every day. Living life with a brain injury, she has overcome and risen above incredible and difficult challenges.

In 2009 she became a member of Brain Injury Services. Since joining Brain Injury Services, she has participated in the PALS Program and Speakers Bureau. She has focused on using her tragic accident into something positive and life-changing for others. Working with Brain Injury Services and the Speakers Bureau, she has regained the confidence she once had. The Speakers Bureau has given her the opportunity to travel throughout the

Northern Virginia area sharing her triumphant story and inspiring everyone she comes in contact with.

Most importantly she educated people on brain injury and how to care for a brain injury survivor. LaToya partnered up with Total Life Changes also known as TLC, a health and wellness company. After suffering during 8 years of excruciating pain, TLC products were able to keep her pain free. Something that prescription medicine has never been able to do. She had to be apart of an amazing company that changes people lives all around the world.

LaToya was adopted in the Army Of Angels, a nonprofit organization, that advocating for and finding support for those experiencing domestic violence. Being a survivor of domestic violence, which is the main reason she became an activist and speaking out about her experiences with others. The Army Of Angels is a perfect fit for her to be apart of. LaToya enjoys assisting in

helping organize fundraisers and different events for the Army of Angels.

LaToya has been participating in domestic violence events by speaking on the different panels for Women Of Excellence, Love By The Handles, and the 2nd Breaking Free Forever conference. She has the pleasure to be a featured author for the book anthology for this conference and plans to tour throughout the country and international promoting the book.

She is pleased to be apart the 5% of people who survive being shot in the head. But extremely grateful to be one 3% of people who live an independent life. LaToya is honored to be uses by God to be an example of faith, miracles and nothing is impossible for God. Her hopes and dreams is to inspire and educate young women & men and hoping they will learn from her choices.

ABOUT THE VISIONARY

Da'Mali T. Goings-Rector graciously known as "Minister Rector" is an inventive humble servant whose life emulates a true giving spirit evangelizing a resounding message of hope and recognizing self-worth while living a life of love intentionally on purpose. A mother of three, Certified Lay Minister, Speaker, and Author, Da'Mali is known for her love, dedication, and commitment to those she serves.

With over 19 years in the "customer service" industry and many years in ministry, she incorporates her love and cares for people while bringing a powerful message that resonates in the hearts of those she connects with leaving the imprint of God's love on their hearts. Her passion and promotion of complete wellness (mental, spiritual, emotional, social, and physical) help build balance and wholeness inside and outside the walls of the church.

In 2009, she became certified as a CLM (Certified Lay Minister) in the United Methodist Church and in 2017 received certification in Health Ministry through Wesley Theological School and attended Lancaster Bible College with a focus in Biblical Studies.

As an advocate, Da'Mali uses her voice to fight for the acknowledgement of rights for domestic violence survivors and she also helps to provide resources, education and support to help eradicate domestic violence in homes and communities by serving as the President of the Board of Directors for Love By the Handles, a 501(c)3 organization based in Washington, DC.

She has received numerous awards and acknowledgments such as the 2016 Metro Phenomenal Woman Award and has been able to reach an audience of women through her writing projects The Groove Never Stops-Stories of Intense Determination and Breaking Free Forever: The Momentous Journey.

She loves studying and meditating on the word of God and one of her favorite scriptures is Romans 8:18 "For I consider [from the standpoint of faith] that the sufferings of the present life are not worthy to be compared with the glory that is about to be revealed to us and in us!" and her favorite quote is by Dr. Maya Angelou, "Life is not measured by the breaths we take but by the moments that take our breath away"

No matter the accomplishments, Da'Mali just wants to be recognized as a child and servant of God as she works in the vineyard gleaning souls for Christ!